The Homilist's Guide
to Scripture,
Theology, and Canon Law

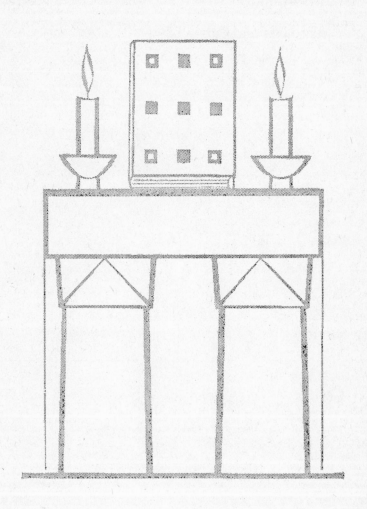

John Burke, O.P. and Thomas P. Doyle, O.P.

The Homilist's Guide to Scripture, Theology, and Canon Law

Pueblo Publishing Company

New York

Nihil Obstat:
Rev. J.A. DiNoia, O.P.
Censor Deputatus

Imprimatur:
Rev. Msgr. Raymond Boland
Vicar General, Archdiocese of Washington

December 1, 1986

The nihil obstat and imprimatur are official declarations that a book or pamphlet is free of doctrinal or moral error. No implication is contained therein that those who have granted the nihil obstat and the imprimatur agree with the content, opinions or statements expressed.

Design: Frank Kacmarcik

Contents

Introduction

This book, *The Homilist's Guide to Scripture, Theology, and Canon Law*, explores the preaching ministry scripturally, theologically, canonically, and pastorally. That is, for each aspect of the preaching ministry, we hope to explain its scriptural foundation, its theological articulation in the tradition of the Church, the legislation of the Church, and the reasons for that legislation. In addition, we will be treating the very practical matters that result, not only from these factors, but also from the nature of oral communication itself, of which preaching is one form.

Preaching, however, is not merely the communication of information, but the handing on of faith: "Thus faith comes from what is heard, and what is heard comes through the word of Christ" (Rom 10:17). Lay persons as well as clergy share in this ministry: parents, lay catechists, youth ministers, counselors, and the like. In fact, Canon 766 of the new *Code of Canon Law* explicitly authorizes lay persons to preach under certain circumstances, even permitting them to preach in churches and oratories. Although their entire ministry is subject to the prescriptions of the conference of bishops, the only restriction imposed upon the laity by the Law in the exercise of their ministry is that they may not preach the homily at the Eucharist.

Although the laity have always had a fundamental and constant role in the transmission of the faith, the code's provision for lay preaching marks a significant departure from recent custom and legislation. Lay preaching holds tantalizing possibilities for the future of the Church in the United States. Because there will be an acute shortage of priests—until now the usual ministers of the word—necessity alone will make lay preaching a major factor in the communication of the gospel message.

It is hoped that this book will be read by all who exercise the ministry of the word in any way: bishops, priests and deacons, as well as lay persons.

To be effective in sharing faith, preachers can only speak from faith. In the act of preaching the word of God, therefore, preachers are really communicating their own experience of God's saving power in their lives. Speaking of faith from faith constitutes the act of preaching that has the power to change the hearts of men and women and bring them into union with God himself.

Because to preach is to participate in the power of the Divine Wisdom, preachers do not preach in their own name. They can only preach in the name of the Church by whom they are sent. Consequently, the word that they preach must necessarily be one with the teaching of the Church. They use their own words and shape the teaching in the light of their experience, yet the teaching they communicate, if it is to be true and effective preaching, is necessarily the teaching of the Church.

THE OFFICE OF PREACHING

All of Christ's faithful (*Christifideles*) share in the right and obligation of the teaching office of Christ, each according to his or her particular status in the Church.

Some preach by their teaching and catechizing, whereas others participate in the formal office of preaching. Herein lies the basis for an important distinction: while all of the faithful, by their baptism, share in the obligation to spread the gospel, certain of the faithful, because of their status, have the office of preaching.

The Supreme Pontiff holds the fullness of the office of preaching, which means that the Pope ultimately regulates and accepts responsibility for the communication of the divine message. As successors to Peter and the other apostles, the Pope and the bishops in communion with him exercise the office of preaching by the Divine Will Itself (c. 386, 1; 756, 1). In the day-to-day life of the Church, those to whom the office of preaching has been entrusted necessarily share it with others with whom they collaborate.

There can be no question that the office and ministry of preaching is essential to the communication of the word of Christ and, therefore, to the life and welfare of the Church. Hence, the Church regulates not only what can be formally preached, but it also determines who can share in this ministry. All Christians have the right and obligation to spread the gospel of Jesus Christ as it is communicated through His body, the Church. In this way, they make disciples of all nations as Christ commanded (Mt 28:19).

THE CHURCH LAW ON PREACHING

The Church law on preaching is found in a number of places in the new *Code of Canon Law*. The fundamental norms are in Book III, Title I, Chapter I. This entire book of the Code is devoted to the "Teaching Office of the Church." Preeminent among the means of teaching is preaching. There are also indirect references to preaching in the canons that treat the basic rights and obligations of the faithful in Book II, "The People of God." Preaching is also referred to in subsequent canons concerned with the duties attached to specific offices and ministries in the Church. Finally, there is mention of preaching in numerous places in the normative sections of the liturgical books and in several legislative or exhortative documents issued by the Holy See (for example, *Inaestimabile donum* of 1980).

This book, therefore, seeks to explore the consequences of this new legislation for ordinary pastoral activity on the diocesan and parish level. The formulation of the new law for the Church requires the setting of new priorities both in the preparation for and the actual exercise of ministry.

In this book, we have elected to use the usual inclusive English language structure: unless the sense clearly indicates to the countrary, all masculine references include women: man, mankind, he, his, etc.

These introductory remarks are drawn to a close by reminding our readers that Church law on preaching exists to help the preacher and the faithful and is not meant to hinder them from hearing the word of the Lord. And so, with the publication of this work, go our sincere prayers that the Holy Spirit will enlighten our readers as they explore the preaching ministry in the Church today. This prayer is joined with that of the author of the Letter to the Ephesians for his beloved Church at Ephesus:

"That he [the Father of our Lord, Jesus Christ] may grant you in accord with the riches of his glory to be strengthened with power through his Spirit in the inner self, and that Christ may dwell in your hearts through faith; that you, rooted and grounded in love, may have strength to comprehend with all the holy ones what is the breadth and length and height and depth, and to know the love of Christ that surpasses knowledge, so that you may be filled with all the fullness of God" (Eph 3:16–19).

John Burke, O.P.
Thomas P. Doyle, O.P.

Chapter One

A Working Definition of Preaching

All of the Church's earthly efforts tend toward effecting the salvation of the world.[1] The Church does this through preaching the word and celebrating the sacraments. Preaching, as we have seen in the Introduction, is a form of teaching—a role that is fundamental to the Church's existence.

By looking at the Church's legislation, both past and present, we can see that the Church has always considered preaching to be one of the most important aspects of its ministry. Preaching is more than commenting on a gospel passage or giving an informative instruction on Church doctrine. It is the transmission of the faith.

Generically, preaching means teaching the gospel and ✓ inciting people not only to believe in it but to live it. This duty has been principally committed to the Supreme Pontiff for the universal Church and to the bishops for the particular or local churches (c. 756). The Church's right to regulate preaching, both as to content and to those who exercise the office, is grounded in its power to teach.

Those familiar with Church law will know that the 1917 *Code of Canon Law* also contained legislation related to the preaching and teaching of the word. In fact, throughout its history, the Church, through its leaders, has enacted legislation about preaching in re-

sponse to its obligation to protect the transmission of
the word of God.

PREACHING IN THE LAW

The First Millenium
From the time of the primitive Church (first to third
centuries), preaching has formed an integral part of
the liturgical worship, as it does today. Even in the
primitive Church, the bishops were recognized as having both the principal duty to preach themselves and
also the duty to regulate the preaching of others. As
the infant Church quickly grew, the bishops relied
more and more on the priests and deacons in the exercise of the teaching ministry. Bishops empowered
priests, deacons, and even laymen to preach the homily, which was the dominant form of preaching.[2]

Synods and councils of the early Church contain instances of legislation on preaching. Much of this legislation concerned who could preach and where they
could preach. For instance, the Council of Chalcedon
(ca. 451) forbade monks to preach outside their monas-
teries, and the Apostolic Constitutions of about 380 forbade women to preach. One other interesting piece of
legislation points up the perennial nature of pastoral
problems. The "Ancient Statutes of the Church" in a
passage attributed to the Council of Carthage (ca. 398)
forbade the faithful, under pain of excommunication,
from leaving the Church while the bishop was
preaching.

It is striking that even from the earliest centuries
Church legislation was needed to remind and urge the
bishops, priests, and deacons of their duty to preach.
These laws related the duty to preach to the need of
the people to hear the word of the Lord. The Council
of Toledo (ca. 655), for instance, commanded that the
bishops not only preach, but devote themselves to

2

study of the Scriptures lest their charges suffer from hunger for the word.

Some interesting accommodations were made in those times. If the bishop was indisposed or not available, the priests were to preach; for this reason, they were to be given faculties to do so in the cities and outlying areas. At this same time (seventh century), if the priests were not available, the deacons were to read from the sermons of the Church Fathers, thus providing the faithful with a form of preaching.

Other legislation from the first millenium of Christian history treats the content of preaching. The bishops and priests could not say whatever came to mind or whatever they felt was appropriate. They had a dual responsibility: to the word and to the faithful. The Synod of Liege (ca. 710) directed preachers to proclaim the commandments and to teach what was necessary for salvation. The Council of Frankfort (794) decreed that the people be taught the essential doctrines of the creed and the prayers. A document drawn up by Charlemagne in 802 listed the subjects that were to be preached. They included the prayers, basic truths, and explanations of the worship services.

To fully understand the legislation of this early period during the Dark Ages, one must understand that the Church was in a continual state of flux. The Roman empire had disintegrated and was now subject to the migrating Germanic tribes. There was general social disorder and very little development of the arts or scholarship in these latter centuries of the first millenium. The Church was not centrally organized and was, in great part, engaged in a kind of primitive missionary enterprise. Whereas the Church had to rely on the communication of its truths and on its worship services for its very existence, many or most of the clergy, while motivated by good will, were ill-educated and, therefore, unable to fulfill their duties as competent preachers.

Legislation was passed to make the bishops overcome their laxity in preaching, and the most ignorant priests were prohibited from preaching. The state of homiletics in the eighth-century Frankish kingdom was obviously a far cry from that of the age of St. Augustine, if the legislative sources are any indication. Thousands of erudite sermons of Augustine and the other early Fathers were preserved, portions of which were and are still used in the Divine Office. Yet by the eighth century, it was necessary to enact laws to ensure that the priests at least understood the meaning of the Our Father and did not fabricate teachings out of their own ignorance.

The High Middle Ages
Preaching was perhaps at its lowest ebb at the end of the eleventh century. This is not difficult to imagine if one looks at the overall deplorable state of the Church. Yet western civilization took a turn for the better with the beginning of what is sometimes referred to as the High Middle Ages, a period that began in the twelfth century and stretched to the end of the thirteenth century at least. The arts, scholarship, and society in general experienced a rebirth. The universities flourished as centers of secular and religious learning, and the papacy expanded its power and prestige.

There were also dark clouds on this otherwise bright horizon, for heresy effective enough to attract significant numbers of followers developed in this same period. Some of the heresies can be connected with the poor quality of preaching. At the time of the Fourth Lateran Council (ca. 1215) unauthorized preachers, usually laymen, had been promoting their doctrines, while the clergy were still lax about preaching, espe-

4

cially at Mass. Groups such as the Waldenses and the Humiliati claimed a right to preach without ecclesiastical approval, citing the Scriptures or early Christian practices as their justification.

The lower clergy were still generally poorly educated. The higher clergy, such as the bishops and abbots, while much better educated, were often deeply involved in the political life of the times and paid scant attention to such duties as preaching.

The Mandate To Preach

In spite of the deplorable quality of preaching by those who spoke with the Church's authority, the institutional Church was better equipped to rectify the situation than were the unauthorized groups. Ecclesiastical authorities now had to deal with the double problem of poor preaching by official preachers and heretical preaching by unapproved preachers. Church authorities responded with rather direct legislation.

At Lateran Council IV, Pope Innocent III declared that preaching could be done only with the authority of the Pope or other prelate. The same council excommunicated those who presumed to preach without proper authority, no matter how godly their motives. Similar legislation was also enacted at local synods and councils. Finally, at the Council of Constance (fifteenth century) under Pope Martin V, the belief that a priest or deacon was authorized and, indeed, had a right to preach by the very fact of ordination was corrected. The Council decreed that the authority to preach came from the duly constituted Church authorities.

The Friars as Preachers

The most significant development in preaching in the medieval Church was the founding of the preaching friars. The Franciscans were founded in 1207 and enjoyed the papal approval to preach penance, poverty, and morality. The Dominicans, founded especially to preach against heresy, were approved as a religious order in 1215. They were founded in reaction to the heresies rampant in southern France at the time, notably Albigensianism. The bishops needed the assistance of educated preachers and were at a loss to find them from among their own clergy.

The preaching friars were unusual because they received directly from the Pope their authority to preach anywhere. They did not depend on the permission of the local bishops, a point that caused no small amount of friction between the friars and the local clergy. Historical documents recount numerous disputes over the friars' preaching privileges, which were usually referred to Church tribunals. Pope John XXII was prompted to declare that such cases be tried quietly, briefly and without public procedure, thus avoiding polarization of the already existing problems with their resultant scandal.

The Protestant Reformation and the Council of Trent
The Protestant Reformation brought new attitudes toward the authority to preach. One held that the universality of the priesthood entitled anyone to preach according to the "Spirit" without any hampering by Church authority. Another, the concept of the "free pulpit," denied any need of canonical mission in order to be a true minister of the word of God or the sacraments.

The Council of Trent (sixteenth century) in its twenty-fourth session took up the need for the reform of preaching. The authority of the bishops to authorize preaching was reasserted, as was the bishops' solemn duty to preach in their own cathedrals and to see to it that their priests preached in their own churches as well.

The preaching friars' privileges were somewhat curtailed because of the abuses that had occurred as a result of their freedom. They, too, needed the authorization of the local bishop to preach in churches other than their own. Most importantly, the friars needed the approval of their superiors to preach, and the superiors were bound to examine their subjects on the probity of their lives and on their knowledge of and adherence to the Church's doctrine.

Not only were the friars required to have a proper theological education, but so also were the diocesan clergy. The Council of Trent completely reformed the manner in which the clergy were educated and raised to sacred orders. It decreed that only those candidates could be ordained who had been properly prepared, duly examined, and found capable of adequately preaching to the people.

Finally, the Council of Trent approved a catechism, popularly known as the Roman Catechism. This work, a compendium of dogmatic, sacramental, and moral theology, had been drawn up under the strictest scrutiny for the use of priests in preaching and instructing. Its influence continued even into the twentieth century.

If we consider the Church's concern for personal fitness in conjunction with its ever-present concern for doctrinal orthodoxy, we can easily see that preaching is a personal sharing of orthodox faith.

A DEFINITION OF PREACHING IN THE NEW CODE
With the lessons of history in mind, we turn to the legislation now in force to seek a contemporary definition of preaching. As we will see, the present legislation is quite similar in all of the essential aspects to that which has come down from the past.

Preaching is first of all an office (c. 756, 1). Thus, according to Canon 145, it is a stable post established by divine law or ecclesiastical disposition for a spiritual purpose. By *divine* law, this office is held by the Pope and the bishops as the ordinary teachers of the faith (c. 756). By *ecclesiastical* law, the faculty to preach, which is a sharing in the bishops' office is presumed for priests and deacons (c. 764).

The subject of all preaching is basically the gospel (cc. 756 and 757) or the mystery of Christ. That the content of preaching must be in accord with the Church's authentic teaching is clear from another canon:

"The mystery of Christ is to be faithfully and fully presented in the ministry of the Word, which must be founded on Sacred Scripture, Tradition, liturgy and the *magisterium* and life of the Church" (c. 760).

The purpose of preaching is to impart knowledge and to move the hearers to faith:

" . . . to set out those things which it is necessary to believe and to practice for the glory of God and the salvation of all" (c. 758, 1).

The law is not only concerned for the welfare of believers; it is also concerned for the evangelization of those who have not yet heard the word of God. Consequently, the office of preaching includes the obligation to reach out to those who do not believe, for they are also included in the care of souls (c. 771, 2).

Thus far, then, we have seen that preaching is not an occasional occupation undertaken at the pleasure or convenience of the preacher. Rather it is a stable office in the Church for announcing the word of God to believers and nonbelievers alike with the intent of informing them of the articles of faith and inciting them to live and practice the message of Jesus. This office has been instituted by Christ in the Church, and it is legitimate Church authority that is charged with the responsibility of safeguarding through law and regulations the office of preaching.

The canons on the formation of clerics contain legislation on their spiritual and doctrinal preparation. Clerics

"with their own faith founded on and nourished by this teaching, . . . ought to be able properly to proclaim the Gospel to the people of their own time, in a fashion suited to the manner of the people's thinking" (c. 248).

PREACHING IS ORAL COMMUNICATION

Whatever specific form it takes, at root, preaching is the oral communication of the word of God that gives birth to and nourishes faith in God the Father, through Jesus Christ, by the power of the Holy Spirit.

There are two correlative terms, therefore, in preaching that need to be explored: the word of God proclaimed and the faith-trust that the word evokes in the heart of the hearer in response to that proclamation.[3]

THE WORD OF GOD

The "word of God" is the phrase Scripture uses to describe God's communication of his will and power when he brings into being those things that he seeks to create and accomplish. In Isaiah God says:

"So shall my word be
  that goes forth from my mouth;
It shall not return to me void,
  but shall do my will,
  achieving the end for which I sent it" (Is 55:11).

The opening scene of the Bible shows God's word operating in the creation of the world when "God said, 'Let there be light,' and there was light" (Gn 1:3).

Scripture also uses the phrase "word of God" as a very personal expression of God's wisdom and love. This word is spoken in a variety of ways and circumstances in both the Old and New Testaments.

The Old Testament

In the Old Testament, God revealed his endless love and guiding wisdom to his chosen people through the preaching of his inspired prophets who shaped a people by their exhortations, curses, and blessings. The greatest prophet, Moses, laid the foundations for the Jewish people that have lasted to this day. Through the observance of the Law given to Moses on Mt. Sinai, the Hebrews lived in continuing awareness of God's presence and provident care.

The psalmist rejoices in God's guidance and even his presence through his word when he sings:

"I am attacked by malicious persecutors
    who are far from your law.
You, O Lord, are near,
    and all your commands are permanent.
Of old I know from your decrees,
    that you have established them forever"
    (Ps 119:150–2).

The New Testament

The New Testament develops a sophisticated theology of the word of God. The Letter to the Hebrews sums up the word of God as the total teaching of God to his people in both Old Testament and New Testament times. It says:

"In times past, God spoke in partial and various ways to our ancestors through the prophets; in these last days, he spoke to us through a son, whom he made heir of all things and through whom he created the universe" (Heb 1:1,2).

Subsequently, the Letter to the Hebrews describes the word of God as a personification of the divine:

"Indeed, the word of God is living and effective, sharper than any two-edged sword, penetrating even between soul and spirit, joints and marrow, and able to discern reflections and thoughts of the heart. No creature is concealed from him, but everything is naked and exposed to the eyes of him to whom we must render an account" (Heb 4:12,13).

The process of personifying the word of God, which began in the Old Testament (cf. Prv 8:22 ff.; Wis 7:22 ff.), reaches completion in the New, where the Gospel of John identifies Jesus as the word of God made flesh:

"In the beginning was the Word,
    and the Word was with God,
    and the Word was God.
. . . .
And the Word became flesh
    and made his dwelling among us,
    and we saw his glory,
    the glory as of the Father's only Son,
    full of grace and truth" (Jn 1:1–14).

As a result of this identification of Jesus as the word of God made flesh who dwelled among us, all Christian preaching centers around the life, ministry, death, and resurrection of Jesus Christ. Jesus is the Good News who brings our salvation.

"You have been born anew, not from perishable but from imperishable seed, through the living and abiding word of God. . . . This is the word that has been proclaimed to you" (1 Pt 1:23–25).

Upon the reception of the Holy Spirit after Jesus' resurrection, the apostles and disciples preached the Good News, and their preaching extended the community founded by Christ, as the Acts of the Apostles so vividly recounts.

The apostolic preaching, however, did not just recount events that happened in the past; it proclaimed a present mystery—"Christ among us, the hope of God's glory."[4] Apostolic preaching reveals how all peoples can participate in that mystery and share in the riches of the Risen Jesus.

The Letter to the Ephesians makes it very clear that the preacher not only proclaims a fact, he dispenses a present power, the mystery of Christ and his Church.

"To me, the very least of all the holy ones, this grace was given, to preach to the Gentiles the inscrutable riches of Christ, and to bring to light for all what is the plan of the mystery hidden from ages past in God who created all things" (Eph 3:8,9).

The Second Vatican Council declares:

"The mystery of the holy Church is manifest in her very foundation, for the Lord Jesus inaugurated her by preaching the good news, that is the coming of God's Kingdom. . . . Those who hear the word with faith and become part of the little flock of Christ (Lk 12:32) have received the kingdom itself. . . . The Church, consequently, equipped with the gifts of her Founder and faithfully guarding his precepts of charity, humility and self-sacrifice, receives the mission to proclaim and to establish among all peoples the kingdom of Christ and of God. She becomes on earth the initial budding forth of that kingdom" (*Dogmatic Constitution on the Church*, No. 5).

Eventually, the apostolic preaching was written down by the early Church and handed on to us in the writings of the New Testament. Yet, even as the early preaching was being written down, it was also being preserved and communicated in nonwritten form under the continual guidance of the Holy Spirit in the Church of Christ. This nonwritten communication is called "sacred tradition." The two forms, written and nonwritten, constitute the divine revelation entrusted to the Church to be communicated to all generations.

The Dogmatic Constitution on Divine Revelation (No. 9) teaches:

"Both sacred tradition and sacred scripture are to be accepted and venerated with the same sense of devotion and reverence. [For] sacred tradition and sacred scripture form one sacred deposit of the word of God, which is committed to the Church."

The Word Today

The word of God, therefore, is not limited to the Bible written in the distant past. The word of God is not a dead letter on a dead page simply to be read and understood abstractly. God has revealed his wisdom, power, and love in order to bring his people into intimate union with himself, in all times and places, forever. Paul tells his community at Corinth how God's word has been written in their hearts by his preaching:

"You are our letter, written on our hearts, known and read by all, shown to be a letter of Christ administered by us, written not in ink but by the Spirit of the living God, not on tablets of stone but on tablets that are hearts of flesh" (2 Cor 3:2,3).

Today, through the preachers of the Church, God's word continues to form the believing community. When the word of God is heard by noble and generous hearts, the word, by its own power, creates new life in the hearers that is expressed by the term "faith." Paul describes this power:

"For I am not ashamed of the gospel. It is the power of God for the salvation of everyone who believes: for Jew first, and then Greek. For in it is revealed the righteousness of God from faith to faith; as it is written, 'The one who is righteous by faith will live' " (Rom 1:16,17).

The Complexity of the Word
The life of faith begotten by the Good News encompasses a series of experiences based on a relationship with God who teaches us the truth. In teaching the truth, God saves because he not only gives his light, he gives the desire and the power to live in that light. As St. Paul says: "God is the one who, for his good purpose, works in you both to desire and to work" (Phil 2:13).

While the intellectual aspects of God's word are fundamental to the authentic communication of revelation, preaching cannot be satisfied with communicating only information, be it dogma, doctrine or morality. In order to communicate the word of God through preaching, the preacher, whether a homilist, an evangelist, or catechist, needs to take into account all aspects of the word that he preaches.

For example, Sunday preaching cannot be effective when the homily is limited to an exegesis of the scriptural text. Again, when a catechist is satisfied with simply teaching the questions and answers of a catechism, faith will probably not be aroused in his students' hearts. Whereas doctrine is part of preaching—an essential part—the awakening and nourishing of faith requires more, which is the reason for Canon 248.[5]

Presupposed in all our discussion of the causality of preaching in regard to faith is an essential and basic presupposition: namely, both the content of faith—

revelation—and the interior assent to that content is the effect of the grace of God. In revealing himself, however, God works through human mediation, such as the preaching of the prophets, apostles and, in our own day, the teaching of the Church.

But always, the actual movement of interior assent can come only from God himself. Without a movement of grace, human free will is unable to assent to what is revealed by preaching. As a result, preachers are required to do all that the nature of both revelation and communication require to be effective in their ministry. At the same time, they must always recognize the sovereign freedom of God to grace those whom he has chosen.

To put it another way: the Christian preacher communicates a divine wisdom given from above and empowered from above that leads to a new way of life:

"We speak God's wisdom, mysterious, hidden, which God predetermined before the ages for our glory, and which none of the rulers of this age knew for, if they had known it, they would not have crucified the Lord of glory. But as it is written:

" 'What eye has not seen, and ear has not heard,
    and what has not entered the human heart,
    what God has prepared for those who love
        him' " (1 Cor 2:7–9).

God's wisdom cannot be preached in rationalistic terms because, as Paul says, they cannot communicate the meaning and life-giving qualities that flow from the crucifixion of Christ. The cross is not an ideology. The cross is God's power to save.

"For Christ did not send me to baptize but to preach the gospel, and not with the wisdom of human eloquence, so that the cross of Christ might not be emptied of its meaning.

"The message of the cross is foolishness to those who are perishing, but to us who are being saved it is the power of God" (1 Cor 1:17,18).

Therefore, while the Christian preacher preaches truth, it is always a truth that is shaped by and expressed in love. It is, in short, the divine affective truth communicated to us by God over centuries through the activity of prophets in the gathering of God's own people.

Only understanding the word of God in the context of divine wisdom—knowledge, love and Spirit—enables us to speak of meaning: divine meaning and human meaning, and the relationship of love between the two.

THE MEANING OF THE WORD OF GOD

For many, the world is meaningless, the result of the random interaction of forces, which although incredibly powerful, lack purpose and design.

So it is with human life. If we are simply at the vortex of forces over which we have no control, if we are plunged up and down on the turbulent waves of events and things that have no mind to direct them into channels to achieve purposes, then human life is meaningless. Sickness, death, tragedy, crisis wear down the human spirit and destroy it; sometimes quickly, sometimes slowly, but always inevitably.

When no evident meaning emerges, humans impose it. Superstition and magic are efforts to establish meaning and control forces that seem to be acting without purpose. Religion has also been perverted when mere things—rivers, storms, bulls—have been credited with an intentionality they do not have but the human mind needs. The result is false gods, lifeless idols.

Preaching Reveals Meaning

The preaching of God's word delivers us from meaninglessness. Preaching reveals the divine purpose behind all events as that purpose has been revealed by the One who has created all things according to his eternal plan. The revelation of the divine purpose begins, of course, with Genesis' account of the creation of the world and, in particular, the creation of men and women. While divine purpose is reaffirmed in many Old Testament texts, the story of Abraham begins a process of greater specification of God's intention. The process is completed only when the ultimate purpose of creation is fully revealed in the preaching of Jesus and the apostles and the writings of the New Testament. In the Letter to the Ephesians, we have a magnificent summary statement of God's intention that gives meaning to all human life:

"He has made known to us the mystery of his will in accord with his favor that he set forth in him as a plan for the fullness of times, to sum up all things in Christ, in heaven and on earth" (Eph 1:9,10).

Not only has God revealed his plan to us, he has revealed how we can unite ourselves with his overarching purpose and thereby find personal peace and happiness. Jesus taught the way to union with the Godhead:

"As the Father loves me, so I also love you. Remain in my love. If you keep my commandments, you will remain in my love, just as I have kept my Father's commandments and remain in his love.

"I have told you this so that my joy might be in you and your joy might be complete. This is my commandment: love one another as I love you. No one has greater love than this, to lay down one's life for one's friends. You are my friends if you do what I command you. I no longer call you slaves, because a slave does not know what his master is doing. I have called you friends, because I have told you everything I have heard from my Father" (Jn 15:9–15).

Insight into Meaning
Insight is a creative act of the intellect and will that originates spontaneously, as it were, within us. Insight is formed in the secret place where we perceive intuitively the unity of creation and experience ourselves as one with it. As a result, there has always been something mysterious and uncontrollable about insight. The ancients called insight the gift of the Muses; Christians recognize insight as the work of the Spirit. Insight is of us and from us, and yet, it is truly beyond us. We know with an intense clarity, and at the same time we wonder how we ever found out.[6]

We become very sensitive to the importance and power of insight when we do not experience it. For example, we may have struggled with a problem for a long time perhaps. We may even have glimmerings of a solution, yet the answer remains just beyond us, and we are powerless to push further on. We can only helplessly wait on insight to express itself and lead us out of our darkness into the wonderful light of truth. In terms of the gospel, when insight comes as a revelation from above, all life is changed. Sometimes the change is great, sometimes less, depending upon the depth of the insight.

In the Second Letter to the Corinthians, Paul speaks of a basic moment of insight when the Lord said to him: "My grace is sufficient for you, for power is made perfect in weakness" (2 Cor 12:9). Up until that point, Paul had been suffering intensely from a mysterious "thorn in the flesh." Prayers for deliverance had been unavailing; then, suddenly, the Lord spoke, insight was given, and Paul's life was changed. From that moment on, Paul was "content with weaknesses, insults, hardships, persecutions, and constraints, for the sake of Christ; for when I am weak, then I am strong" (2 Cor 12:10).

His awareness of God's power in his life was a central theme of all Paul's preaching and was the motivation that enabled Paul to endure a variety of sufferings for the sake of his preaching ministry: persecution, hardships, and insults. Furthermore, the knowledge that God had empowered him to preach, in spite of being an "earthenware jar," drove Paul to proclaim "our Savior Christ Jesus, who destroyed death and brought life and immortality to light through the gospel" in a ceaseless ministry as herald, apostle, and teacher (2 Tm 1:10). Even imprisonment, "his chains," became an occasion for preaching and bearing witness (Eph 6:20).

Indeed, Paul realized that all of his preaching ministry and his ability to proclaim the mystery was the effect of God's grace:

"To me, the very least of all the holy ones, this grace was given, to preach to the Gentiles the inscrutable riches of Christ, and to bring to light for all what is the plan of the mystery hidden from ages past in God who created all things" (Eph 3:8,9).

In short, Paul's insight is expressed in Scripture in Ephesians 2:8–10:

"By grace you have been saved through faith, and this is not from you; it is the gift of God; it is not from works, so no one may boast. For we are his handiwork, created in Christ Jesus for the good works that God has prepared in advance, that we should live in them."

This insight took many different forms in Paul's life, preaching, and writing. Sometimes Paul's awareness of dependence was more intense, sometimes less, as

God pushed him to accomplish the task he had assigned him.[7] But always the recognition of God's generosity sustained Paul and enabled him to endure hardship as well as to enjoy the delights his creation offers the followers of Christ.

Insight also motivates preachers today. Insight urges ministers ever onward to proclaim God's word. Paul gave eloquent expression to that impulse:

"It is Christ in you, the hope for glory. It is he whom we proclaim, admonishing everyone and teaching everyone with all wisdom, that we may present everyone perfect in Christ. For this I labor and struggle, in accord with the exercise of his power working within me" (Col 1: 27b–29).

The Need To Communicate

A desire to communicate—no, more—a *need* to communicate is a key element in creative insight, which is at the heart of preaching. Creativity proceeds in some way from a love that desires to communicate what it knows first hand. Consider contemporary song writers, whether of rock, country, or popular music. They want to communicate meaning; they want their songs to be heard. Their delight in putting their artistic insights into music is not just writing the song—that is an important element, obviously—but they want the song sung, heard, accepted, and loved. They use the song to enter into creative dialogue with an audience, as a writer does with the readers of his words. The creative act invites and expects response, hopefully of agreement, because it seeks to share truth.

Is this not why God communicates with us in the first place? He seeks a response from us—the response of faith. The preacher ministers the creative act of God bringing life to the dead when he preaches the word of God.

"Even when we were dead in our transgressions, [God] brought us to life with Christ (by grace you have been saved), and raised us up with him, and seated us with him in the heavens in Christ Jesus" (Eph 2:5,6).

In preaching, the preacher participates in the creative act of the divine mind, revealing itself to us.

"So whoever is in Christ is a new creation: the old things have passed away; behold, new things have come. And all this is from God" (2 Cor 5:17,18).

The Good News comes from the heart of God—his abundant, abiding love for us. The Good News is an infinite generosity toward all—even toward those who are unworthy of it. The generosity of God is most fully revealed in the cross of Christ, which is why Paul describes the cross as foolishness. Nevertheless, "The foolishness of God is wiser than human wisdom, and the weakness of God is stronger than human strength" (1 Cor 1:25).

At the same time, the cross of Christ is only the beginning of the ongoing revelation of God's love for us in the glorious life of the risen Jesus.

"But God proves his love for us in that while we were still sinners Christ died for us. How much more then, since we are now justified by his blood, will we be saved through him from the wrath. Indeed, if, while we were enemies, we were reconciled to God through the death of his Son, how much more, once reconciled, will we be saved by his life. Not only that, but we also boast of God through our Lord Jesus Christ, through whom we have now received reconciliation" (Rom 5:8–11).

It may seem here that we have departed from properly theological considerations and have become concerned with matter more proper to "spirituality." That is the point. When we seek to communicate the word of God, we necessarily go beyond the order of acquired knowledge and intellectual speculation. We enter into the experience of grace.[8] William J. Hill, O.P., speaking of the well-spring of the preacher's inspiration, says:

"The preacher incorporates the articulation of his own new experiences of God's grace into the ongoing narrative that already constitutes living tradition, thereby creatively augmenting the tradition."[9]

The preacher's object is to communicate his insight into the meaning of divine revelation that has come to him as a result of his studying the word of God and the tradition of the Church and that, furthermore, has been verified by his own faith experience. Putting all these elements together in a synthetic process of creative reflection, the preacher is able to discern and treasure the divine purpose in events. More importantly, his words enable his listeners to discern and treasure the divine purpose in the events of their personal and social lives. Think of Jesus' moving call to trust in the providential care of the heavenly Father in all events:

"As for you, do not seek what you are to eat and what you are to drink, and do not worry anymore. All the nations of the world seek for these things, and your Father knows that you need them. Instead, seek his kingdom, and these other things will be given you besides. Do not be afraid any longer, little flock, for your Father is pleased to give you the kingdom" (Lk 12:29–32).

Today, the process of creative faith synthesis is difficult for many. We can see the facts, but we cannot always discern the connection between the facts in a way that leads to new insight. The concentration in modern education has been upon the process of acquiring information and subsequently reflecting successful acquisition of it through tests and dissertations. Educational methodology has scarcely fostered the development of creative insight.

In the same way, theological analysis is going on in seminaries all over the country; the concentration in the training of seminarians is on orthodox understanding rather than on the development of creative insight. Yet, the preacher needs more than theological orthodoxy. He needs insight in order to communicate the full meaning of the gospel for today as it is conditioned by the times in which we are called to live.

Father Raymond E. Brown puts it eloquently when he says:

"One cannot preach unless one rethinks what one has grasped. All the slogans, 'Preach only what is in the Bible,' or, 'Preach only what the Church teaches,' are simplistic if they do not recognize the need for translating what has been received into a new idiom to keep it alive."[10]

The preacher always has to take a fresh look at the gospel realities. He has to be able to bring together into a personal unity his intimate familiarity with the word of God, his understanding of Christian tradition, his theological reflection, his experience of grace, and his sensitivity to the contemporary situation. Out of this personal synthesis of faith, it is to be hoped that the preacher will create effective communications that will enable his listeners to come to grips with the mysteries of God for themselves. What he preaches will be something he can witness to as true because he has verified it by his own personal experience.

The end result of this kind of reflection leading to insight is always, to some extent, a breakthrough in the preacher's understanding of the gospel. The word previously obscure is not only now understood; it has the power to enlighten others.

Furthermore, if the preacher can speak the word of God only under the impetus of grace, his listeners are able to hear the word of God only under the impetus of grace. It follows that the preaching event is a moment of grace for both preacher and listener. It is part of God's own plan of bringing salvation to those he has chosen. No wonder that the preaching of the word of God should always be an exciting experience for both the preacher himself and his hearers.

The Pastoral Document of the American Bishops' Committee on Priestly Formation, *Fulfilled in Your Hearing*, puts the point this way:

"One of the principal tasks of the preacher is to provide the congregation of the faithful with words to express their faith, and with words to express the human realities to which this faith responds. Through words drawn from the Sacred Scriptures, from the Church's theological tradition, and from the personal appropriation of that tradition through study and prayer, the preacher joins himself and the congregation in a common vision" (Chap. I, p. 6).

The Focus of Insight
Insights, such as we have been describing, are deeply influenced by the personality and circumstances of the preacher. In the expression of the insight, there is a revelation of the person and personality of the preacher. Yet the expression of insight should not be misconstrued as mere personal anecdotalism—a telling of autobiographical stories. Insight is concerned with personal ideas, but personal ideas that go to the very heart of the gospel.

We see such personal insight at work in the writings of the apostle Paul. In his Letter to the Romans, for example, Paul has taken the tradition he has received and made it uniquely his own as he strives to share his experience of Christ with the gentiles to whom he has been sent. So, while we learn a great deal about Paul when we read his letters, we learn even more about the gospel. Paul's focus is never on himself; it is always on God.

Theological Pluralism

There has always been a diversity of understandings regarding the meaning of the gospel message. St. Paul himself in his writings to the Corinthian Church found it necessary to appeal for unity in both belief and action:

"I urge you, brothers, in the name of our Lord Jesus Christ, that all of you agree in what you say, and that there be no divisions among you, but that you be united in the same mind and in the same purpose" (1 Cor 1:10).

Yet, pluralism in itself is not evil. Throughout the centuries in both the eastern and western traditions of the Catholic Church, holy men and women have gathered around especially sainted and gifted persons to form religious communities. The life-styles, theological perceptions, spiritual values, and ministries of these communities differ greatly because the communities' observances reflect the different spiritual insights of their founders into the meaning of the gospel. The great variety of religious communities testifies to the diverse ways the Spirit has graced the Church of Christ.

Given the diversity of understanding of the word of God and given the diverse ways the graces that the word communicates have been experienced over the centuries, it is not surprising that the Church today calls its ministers of the gospel back to the "primary and perpetual foundation" of sacred theology: the written word of God and sacred tradition.[11]

In the personal reflection on the Scriptures by its preachers, the Church will be able to find the unity of teaching that can preserve the unity of faith and practice. This is the heart of the preaching ministry.

"Therefore, all the clergy must hold fast to the sacred Scriptures through diligent sacred reading and careful study, especially the priests of Christ and others, such as deacons and catechists, who are legitimately active in the ministry of the word. This cultivation of Scripture is required lest any of them become 'an empty preacher of the word of God outwardly, who is not a listener to it inwardly' since they must share the abundant wealth of the divine word with the faithful committed to them, especially in the sacred liturgy. This sacred Synod earnestly and specifically urges all the Christian faithful, too, especially religious, to learn by frequent reading of the divine Scriptures the 'excelling knowledge of Jesus Christ.' 'For ignorance of the Scriptures is ignorance of Christ' " (*Dogmatic Constitution on Divine Revelation*, No. 25).

FAITH[12]

Preaching: The Purpose of the Church
The Church preaches the word of God, first, to give birth to faith, and then to nourish and strengthen that faith because the primary, basic mission of the Church is to lead all to faith. Thus, the correlative term to the word of God is faith.

There are a number of documents of the Second Vatican Council where this understanding of the mission of the Church is taught. The *Decree on the Church's Missionary Activity* is one of its clearest expressions. This document is concerned with the establishing, or "implanting," of the Church where it has not yet taken root. Consequently, it is directly concerned with the preaching of the gospel because "The chief means of this implantation is the preaching of the gospel of Jesus Christ" (No. 6).

Number 15 of the same decree sums up how Christian community is formed:

"The Holy Spirit, who calls all men to Christ by the seeds of the Word and by the preaching of the gospel, stirs up in their hearts the obedience of faith. When in the womb of the baptismal font he begets to a new life those who believe in Christ, he gathers them into the one People of God which is 'a chosen race, a royal priesthood, a holy nation, a people of his own (1 Pt 2:9).' "

From this, it is evident that everything else the Church does presupposes the existence of faith in the members of the Church, and without faith, they cannot fruitfully participate in its sacramental life.

"The purpose of the sacraments is to sanctify men, to build up the body of Christ, and finally, to give worship to God. Because they are signs, they also instruct. They not only presuppose faith, but by words and objects they also nourish, strengthen, and express it; that is why they are called 'sacraments of faith' " (*Constitution on the Sacred Liturgy*, No. 59).

Because of the necessity of faith that comes from the hearing of the word of God, the *Decree on the Ministry and Life of Priests* enjoins preaching as the very first duty of priests:

"The People of God finds its unity first of all through the word of the living God, which is quite properly sought from the lips of priests. Since no one can be saved who has not first believed, priests, as co-workers with their bishops, have as their *primary duty* the proclamation of the gospel of God to all" (No. 4).

There are two questions closely connected and interrelated but still distinct that merit our attention here: (1) How important is the Church's preaching of the gospel? (2) Is faith necessary for salvation?

How Important Is the Preaching of the Gospel?

All other reasons aside, the Church's preaching of the gospel is of primary importance because it is required by an explicit and direct command of Jesus Christ, according to the Gospel of Mark, who made salvation dependent on faith:

"Go into the whole world and proclaim the gospel to every creature. Whoever believes and is baptized will be saved; whoever does not believe will be condemned" (Mk 16:15,16).

As a result of this evangelical command, whatever other reasons can be brought to bear on the desirability of preaching, the Church has the responsibility of preaching the word of God "whether it is convenient or inconvenient" (2 Tm 4:2).

The *Dogmatic Constitution on the Church* (No. 17) expresses it this way:

"The Church has received from the apostles as a task to be discharged even to the ends of the earth this solemn mandate of Christ to proclaim the saving truth (cf. Acts 1:8). Hence she makes the words of the Apostle her own: 'Woe to me, if I do not preach it [the gospel]!' (1 Cor 9:16)."

Pope Paul VI, in his landmark *Apostolic Exhortation on Evangelization in the Modern World*, forcefully reaffirmed this teaching when he wrote:

"The presentation of the Gospel message is not an optional contribution for the Church. It is the duty incumbent upon her by the command of the Lord Jesus so that people can believe and be saved. This message is indeed necessary. It is unique. It cannot be replaced. . . . It brings with it a wisdom which is not of this world. . . . It merits having the apostle consecrate all his time and all his energies to it and to sacrifice for it, if necessary, even his own life" (No. 5).

In saying this, Pope Paul is drawing on the many examples of the great Christian martyrs who, throughout the centuries, having willingly and joyfully died that the faith might live.

Is Faith Necessary for Salvation?
According to Mark's gospel, the reason Jesus commanded that his gospel be preached was that unless one believed, one would be condemned (Mk 16:16). All the early Christian Church's activity flowed from the conviction that only through faith could sinners be saved. Not only the preaching of the apostles was to give birth to faith, the literary activity of the Church was directed to the same end. The Gospel of John concludes by telling us that the whole reason for the gospels being written was to lead the reader to faith and through faith to eternal life:

"But these are written that you may [come to] believe that Jesus is the Messiah, the Son of God, and that through this belief you may have life in his name" (Jn 20:31).

Numerous texts in Scripture lay heavy stress on the fundamental necessity of faith, which, in turn, requires a turning from sin to the acceptance of the new value structure faith gives. The synoptic gospels begin with a description of the preaching of John the Baptist. He not only prophesied the coming of Jesus, he prepared for his coming by calling for a change of life through repentance.[13]

The Gospel of John, reflecting the conviction of the early Church, attributes to the lips of John the explicit necessity of faith for salvation:

"Whoever believes in the Son has eternal life, but whoever disobeys the Son will not see life, but the wrath of God remains upon him" (Jn 3:36).

Because saving faith results in obedience to the will of the Father,[14] it divides all humankind into the good and bad, just and unjust.[15] Those who reject God's word are in turn rejected by God.[16]

The Gospel of Matthew has a very vivid description of the final judgment. When the net is full, it will be emptied into a basket and the angels will reach into it to sort the good from the bad, tossing the latter "into the fiery furnace, where there will be wailing and grinding of teeth" (Mt 13:48–50).

In Luke 10:22–24, Jesus describes the inestimable picture of his disciples: they have been able to know the Father through the revelation of the Son. And to know the Father, the Gospel of John says, is to have eternal life.[17]

This knowledge of the Father is not destined for everyone, only the chosen, the few, the remnant. Luke 13:22–30 expresses this truth starkly:

"Someone asked him, 'Lord, will only a few people be saved?' He answered them, 'Strive to enter through the narrow gate, for many, I tell you, will attempt to enter it but will not be strong enough' " (Lk 13:23–24).

There is a misunderstanding today among some Catholics that is seriously hampering the preaching ministry, whatever form it takes, or by whomever it is done. There seems to be an underlying belief that faith is not really all that important; that God is so good he would not punish anyone with eternal damnation. Yet, as we have seen from the examination of just a few texts, the fact is that the Bible presents the grace of salvation (the deliverance or rescue from eternal damnation) through faith as a free gift to the chosen that requires and effects a response and results in the fruit of a new life in Christ. Without this life of faith and its fruit of good works, there is condemnation.

While the final eschatological condemnation is clearly the strain running through the gospels, the Pauline letters reveal that condemnation or "the anger of God" is something that human beings are experiencing now in the flesh. Romans 1:18–32 catalogs some of the signs of condemnation.

The first letter to Peter reinforces the idea of judgment and condemnation now as a sign of the ultimate and eternal condemnation of those who deliberately do evil:

"For it is time for the judgment to begin with the household of God; if it begins with us, how will it end for those who fail to obey the gospel of God?

" 'And if the righteous one is barely saved,
    where will the godless and the sinner appear?' "

(1 Pt 4:17,18)

We can update the scriptural list by painful examples from our own days: enslavement to drugs, alcohol abuse, sexual promiscuity, abortion, violence, racial injustice, economic oppression, war, crime. The list goes on and on.

These vices today are not just abstract listings of evil; they result in great harm to the individuals who commit the evil as well as to their victims. Certainly those who live like this already experience condemnation in this world. One hapless person said it succinctly: "Do you know why I don't fear hell? Because I am already living in it!"

To deliver the world through faith from the condemnation it is experiencing now in its own sinfulness is the purpose of the priesthood:

"That men knowingly, freely and gratefully accept what God has achieved perfectly through Christ and manifest it in their whole lives" (*Decree on the Ministry and Life of Priests*, No. 2).

Can One Be Saved Without Being in the Church?
Although salvation culminates in an eschatological event, salvation begins on earth. Salvation is not only a matter of going to heaven. Salvation is participation in the life of Christ now, while still in the flesh.[18] Salvation begins with entrance into the chosen people of God,[19] the Church, which is an eschatological community of faith.[20] Through entrance into the chosen people, the believer becomes a member of Christ's body.[21]

The preacher identifies the graces or gifts at work in the believer's life. Because God's actions in human beings are far beyond our comprehension, the preacher can only proclaim what God has revealed. The preacher, therefore, can only address himself to those whom God has chosen to hear him (cf. Jn 6:44). The preacher proclaims the message publicly to all, however, because we human beings cannot identify those whom God has chosen. Ultimately, those who do not seem to respond to the divine message must be left to the mercy of God who alone is the judge of the living and the dead.

Once in the community begotten by faith, the believer's personal sins are both borne and forgiven by Christ.[22] In the community, too, Christ communicates his presence, power, and life to the believer, especially through the Holy Eucharist. Because of the riches of the graces given through the ministry of the Church, the believer is able to grow in divine, gospel wisdom.[23]

Furthermore, because gospel wisdom is eminently practical, the believer is given through faith a new power to live according to the light shining from the cross and to bear fruit in the practice of love, as Christ loved on his cross.

The salvation that faith brings, therefore, is a present reality that can be experienced on earth as well as eschatologically in heaven, because, ultimately, living in love, both here and hereafter, constitutes salvation. It is called salvation because, as the entire evidence of human experience attests, the stable, long-lasting love that brings happiness does not seem to be within the natural capacity of man. He needs God's wisdom and power to save him from the evil tendencies in the human heart that impede or even prevent a person from loving: pride, selfishness, greed, etc. (cf. Rom 1:29,30; Gal 5:19–21). In the Christian tradition, some of these blocks have come to be known as the seven capital sins.

Nonetheless, the Church recognizes that God can accomplish his saving work in ways that may not bring the human object of his love into explicit union with the Church:

"Those also can attain to everlasting salvation who through no fault of their own do not know the gospel of Christ or his Church, yet sincerely seek God and, moved by grace, strive by their deeds to do his will as it is known to them through the dictates of conscience. Nor does divine Providence deny the help necessary for salvation to those who, without blame on their part, have not yet arrived at an explicit knowledge of God, but who strive to live a good life, thanks to his grace" (*Dogmatic Constitution on the Church*, No. 16).

Romans 2:12–16 provides the scriptural source for this teaching. In this passage, Paul says that the virtuous nonbeliever pagan who lives according to his conscience, even though he may not have faith, can still look forward to having some justification for his way of life when "God will judge people's hidden works through Christ Jesus" (Rom 2:16). The importance of living according to one's conscience, even if one has not been given faith to live by, constitutes a major moral principle for Paul. This principle is valid because God is the author of both faith and reason; even though one does not have faith, God has engraved in the human heart a certain understanding of and tendency to do good. The "Law" makes explicit what was implicit in the human heart.

"For when the Gentiles who do not have the law by nature observe the prescriptions of the law, they are a law for themselves even though they do not have the law" (Rom 2:14).

Furthermore, the Bible recognizes that not everyone has fullness of faith. For whatever reason, there are those who have only a minimal understanding of God and their relationship to him. Nevertheless, even this minimal level of faith establishes a personal relationship to a saving God who knows and loves, and this relationship is adequate for salvation. It is enough to believe that God "exists and that he rewards those who seek him" (Heb 11:6).

Explicit faith, on the other hand, is certainly to be desired and striven for. Explicit faith, as described, for example in Ephesians 2:1–10, makes the believer one of God's works of art and empowers him to live "for the good works that God has prepared in advance" (Eph 2:10).

There are two further levels of faith that are taught explicitly in the Bible: Mark 16:16, previously cited, requires the reception of baptism, and John 6:53 teaches that the reception of the Eucharist is essential for eternal life:

"Jesus said to them, 'Amen, amen, I say to you, unless you eat the flesh of the Son of Man and drink his blood, you do not have life within you. Whoever eats my flesh and drinks my blood has eternal life, and I will raise him on the last day' " (Jn 6:53,54).

For Catholics, these biblical teachings mandate active participation in the entire sacramental life of the Church. Nevertheless, they clearly teach that God's merciful and saving action is not limited to formal participation in the Church. God is always sovereignly free to act outside the channels of grace he has willed to make normative for his saving help.

NOTES

1. "Salvation of the world" is certainly an all-embracing reality. It spans all of human existence because salvation begins on earth, yet is fully realized only in eternity. The human being, once given life by God will live forever, and his joyful union with God that begins on earth will never end.

Salvation, which is ultimately final and eternal union with God, is accomplished through a variety of causes and produces a variety of intermediate effects. The complexity of how God effects this union with his creatures is evident from the complexity of the revelation that makes known both God's intention to save and the means by which God has chosen to bring it about.

In the pages that follow, salvation will be approached from a variety of perspectives, each attempting to make clear the specific aspect of the saving work of God under discussion. To assist the reader in following the arguments being proposed, certain distinctions are made that should be understood when referring to the particular facets of grace as they are described subsequently.

Since salvation is beyond the natural power of the human person to attain, it is called a grace. That is, it is a "supernatural" reality that God gives to human beings because he freely wills to do so. It is not something that flows from their nature as human, unlike for example, the power to digest food or work mathematical problems.

Supernatural grace in its ultimate sense is God himself (Uncreated Grace), with whom the "saved" person is united by the created graces God bestows on his chosen ones.

To effect salvation, God causes in the human person certain qualitative changes in the innermost being—soul—of the person. The most radical change is effected by sanctifying grace, which affects the very essence of the person and makes him pleasing to God. This basic change finds expression, as it were, in the habitual graces that constitute the various intellectual and moral virtues (including especially the theological virtues of faith, hope, and love) and the gifts of the Holy Spirit.

Actual graces are those special movements of God in the soul that prepare the person to receive sanctifying grace and habitual graces (prevenient grace) or enable him to follow the effects that sanctifying the habitual graces produce in the soul (subsequent grace).

God effects these internal changes in the human person that constitute the essence of salvation through certain external causes or graces. These include such directly supernatural causes as divine revelation in Scripture, tradition, preaching, or divine power communicated through the sacraments, and miracles. Always, however, the effectiveness of these external graces depends on the interior movements of grace in the heart and mind of humans that only God himself can cause.

But God also leads his chosen ones to salvation through the ordinary events of their lives which dispose them to receive sanctifying grace. Providential disposition of events, new understandings, reactions in moments of crisis would be examples of such dispositions. This kind of grace is called prevenient grace because sanctification has not yet taken place but is being prepared for.

God also bestows another kind of grace that is given, not for the sanctification of the individual, but for the sanctification of the Church. These graces are called the charismatic graces (*gratiae gratis datae*) and include such effects as speaking in tongues, healing, discernment of spirits, and the like.

For more extensive treatment of this subject, see St. Thomas Aquinas, *Summa Theologiae*, I–II, qq. 109–114; also Reginald Garrigou-LaGrange, O.P., *Grace: A Commentary on the Summa Theologiae of St. Thomas Aquinas*, I–II, qq.109–114, trans. by Dominican Nuns, Corpus Christi Monastery (St. Louis: B. Herder Book Co., 1957).

2. Jos. Allgeier, *The Canonical Obligation of Preaching in Parish Churches* (Washington, DC: Catholic University of America Press, 1949), pp. 3–6.

3. Faith is a form of habitual grace that makes an individual pleasing to God because it relates him to God as one who accepts what God has revealed and puts his trust in him as his Father.

Faith, precisely because it always exceeds human power, is a gift from God; yet, the gift is bestowed in a variety of ways. Because it is in the nature of a supernatural and habitual grace, it requires dispositions of soul in order to receive it; hence, it requires prevenient or dispositive grace. This accounts for the experience of many converts who testify to their awareness of God's movement in their lives even before they had the vocabulary to express what was happening to them.

Preaching, and Scripture and tradition on which it is based, are external graces that reveal the Trinitarian Godhead, a reality that could never have been known by the unaided human mind. Jesus himself, of course, is the greatest of the external graces because he is God-made-flesh, Grace Incarnate.

While these external graces specify the object of faith—the divine persons—the assent of faith itself always requires an interior movement of grace by the Holy Spirit.

4. Cf. Colossians 1:27.

5. *Supra,* p. 9.

6. In keeping with the distinctions we have made previously, we can see that an insight can be either natural or supernatural. All insights, like all natural knowledge, depend on the divine premotion; yet, that would not be sufficient reason to call an insight a grace. Certainly, artists are gifted people, in the sense that they have received from their Creator certain natural talents that result in insight.

The preacher, on the other hand, seeks to penetrate more deeply into the meaning of supernatural realities; hence, his work at core is supernatural because it deals with matters that can be known only by revelation. Granted that he deals with revelation, a preacher can have insight into it that is simply the result of his natural giftedness. Some preachers, however, have the experience of penetrating into what has been revealed in a way that far exceeds their natural talents, at least as far as they can determine them. Such seems to happen to those preachers who have an unusual sensitivity to the needs of their audiences and, consequently, are able to preach in a way that enables the listener to understand the gospel message with great clarity, particularly as it affects their personal lives.

Finally, however, there are those preachers who have a depth of insight into meaning that is truly miraculous. They are enabled by God to read the hearts of their fellow human beings in order to see precisely what God has in mind for their happiness. The great saints are frequently credited with such supernatural insights, for example, St. John Vianney, whose preaching was clearly more the result of grace than natural talent.

7. Cf. 1 Corinthians 9:16.

8. A question that has run throughout Christian tradition is: How much can a human being know about God without

needing special grace? Or to put it another way: Where does nature leave off and supernature begin?

Debated as the question has been by the greatest minds, one answer, which reflects the substance of the conclusion of the debate, is accepted here: We cannot know for sure. The harmonious interacting of God's creation, natural, supernatural, physical, moral, and spiritual, is so perfect that the limited human mind simply cannot identify the distinctive causes and effects that reflect the divine glory.

9. "What is Preaching? One Heuristic Model from Theology" in *A New Look at Preaching*, ed. by John Burke, O.P. (Wilmington, DE: Michael Glazier, Inc., 1983), p. 119.

10. "Preaching in the Acts of the Apostles" in *A New Look at Preaching*, op. cit., p. 73.

11. *Dogmatic Constitution on Divine Revelation*, No. 24.

12. See Note 3, this chapter.

13. Matthew 3:1-12; Mark 1:1-8; and Luke 3: 3:18.

14. Matthew 7:21-27.

15. Psalm 1.

16. Matthew 10:14,15; and Mark 8:38.

17. John 17:3.

18. John 14:19,20.

19. John 10:16; and 1 Peter 2:9.

20. 2 Thessalonians 2:13-3:5.

21. 1 Corinthians 12:12-30.

22. Ephesians 3:13-14.

23. 1 Corinthians 12:1-13:13.

Chapter Two

The Church's Obligation To Preach

FUNDAMENTAL OBLIGATION TO PREACH
The 1983 *Code of Canon Law* emphasizes the universal
need for human beings to hear authentic preaching in
all cultures, times, and countries. This fact also implies
the Church's obligation to preach. Canon 747 summarizes both the right and obligation of the Church:

"It is the obligation and inherent right of the Church,
independent of any human authority, to preach the
gospel to all peoples, using for this purpose even its
own means of social communication; for it is to the
Church that Christ the Lord entrusted the deposit of
faith, so that by the assistance of the Holy Spirit, it
might conscientiously guard revealed truth, more intimately penetrate it and faithfully proclaim and expound it.

"The Church has the right always and everywhere to
proclaim moral principles, even in respect to the social
order, and to make judgments about any human matter in so far as this is required by fundamental human
rights or the salvation of souls" (c. 747).

Considering the serious problems with which the
world confronts believing Christians today and, at the
same time, the longing of people for clear guidance, it
is no wonder that the new *Code of Canon Law* places
such great stress on preaching. Preaching is the essential means by which the Church communicates the gos-

pel of Jesus Christ; therefore its content must be always well-grounded in the Scriptures and in the teaching of the Church. Further, the code also decrees that whereas preaching demands more than accuracy of teaching, preachers must be able to communicate the gospel in a manner that leads to acceptance and commitment on the part of the hearers.

PREACHING AS DEFINED IN THE 1983 CODE

A cursory look at the law on preaching as well as the theological and historical literature on the subject point to the fact that "preaching" has generally been viewed as a generic form of religious activity. There has been and continues to be a tendency to invest preaching with the broadest possible meaning, so as to be able to embrace a wide diversity of interpretations of what preaching is and how it is done.

Yet, in spite of its generic nature, preaching has a very definite meaning. In both the 1917 and 1983 *Codes of Canon Law*, preaching is included in the "Book on the Teaching Office of the Church." Both codes consider preaching to be a form of teaching or imparting of information from one person or body of persons to another individual or group. At the same time, both codes require that preaching should do more than simply inform the hearers of the divine message; both codes expect preaching to empower the hearers to embrace that message in a way that will help them to live better, fuller, and happier lives.

Thus, preaching is neither lecturing nor simply explaining the meaning of the Scriptures; preaching is not just persuasion, dramatic exhortation, or entertainment. None of these activities, however valuable in themselves, can achieve the end of preaching. Canon 762 says preaching results in the formation of the People of God:

"The people of God are first united through the word of the living God, and are fully entitled to seek this word from their priests. For this reason sacred ministers are to consider the office of preaching as of great importance, since proclaiming the Gospel of God to all is among their principal duties."

God's power, his grace, comes to the Church through its members who serve one another according to the gifts they have received:

"He gave some as apostles, others as prophets, others as evangelists, others as pastors and teachers, to equip the holy ones for the work of ministry, for building up the body of Christ" (Eph 4:11,12).

At the basis of this diversified communication of grace in the body of Christ is preaching. It is the fundamental mission of the Church on which all its other activities rest and, indeed, are made possible. The Church's law sees preaching, therefore, as a graced moment in which those mandated by the Church present, explain, persuade, and empower the listeners to envelope themselves in God's word and, thereby, to believe. Jesus said: "If you remain in my word, you will truly be my disciples, and you will know the truth, and the truth will set you free" (Jn 8:31,32). Faith makes the People of God. The gift of faith, imparted by the Father, makes the Church the Body of Christ.

The generic word "preaching," used in the codes of 1917 and 1983, comes from the Latin noun *praedicatio*, which has a number of related meanings, the most basic of which would be "a public proclaiming, a proclamation, a publication." The related verb, *praedico*, means "to make known by crying in public, to announce, declare, praise, commend." We also say sometimes that people preach by their example. The term used in Church law, however, refers to a public proclamation of the word of God in a way that gives birth to and nourishes faith.

The 1917 code had three chapters in the general title on preaching: catechetics, sermons (*De Sacris Concionibus*), and missions. The 1983 code has simplified this material into one general title, "The Ministry of the Divine Word," with two subchapters, "Preaching the Word of God" and "Catechetical Formation," making two divisions: preaching and catechetics. Within the section on preaching, the code makes three divisions: preaching in general, homilies, and parish missions.

THE CHURCH'S RESPONSIBILITY FOR THE OFFICE OF PREACHING

Because preaching provides the foundation for Christian religious experience, the Church has a responsibility both to provide preachers and to guarantee that those whom it provides to preach do so adequately. Thus, it must carefully legislate who may preach in its name. Unlike some Christian denominations for whom an "interior call" is sufficient justification to preach, Canon Law only allows those to do so whom the church officially chooses and empowers. While all Christians have a serious obligation to give witness to the gospel by their lives, all do not have an equal obligation or even a right to preach in the sense that preaching is understood in law and theology.

Furthermore, the law distinguishes the ministry of preaching from the obligation to exercise this ministry. Some members of the Church bear the obligation to preach because of the office they hold. While all others have some basic, common Christian obligation to witness, they may preach only insofar as they are deputed or delegated to preach in response to certain needs in the Church.

In the 1917 code, authority to preach in the name of the Church was called "canonical mission," and, although somewhat modified in Canon 754 of the 1983 code, this concept remains valid today. Ultimately, canonical mission comes from either the Holy See or the Ordinary (resident bishop), both of whom have the right and power to teach by reason of their office. The pertinent canon from the 1917 code reads as follows:

"No one may exercise the ministry of preaching unless he has received a mission from his lawful superior, either by special grant of the faculty to preach, or by receiving an office to which the function of preaching is attached according to canon law" (C.I.C., c. 1328).

Thus, in both codes, the right and duty to preach comes from the ecclesiastical power of governance—jurisdiction—and not from the power of sacred orders. For this reason, the authority to preach is derived from an ecclesiastical office, not from ordination to the priesthood or deaconate.

In Canon Law, preaching is a jurisdictional office[1] that is part of the "munus docendi," or the teaching mission that Christ committed to the Church. Furthermore, the 1917 code restricted the exercise of jurisdiction to those in sacred orders, so that only ordained clergy could hold ecclesiastical offices or receive the delegated faculty to preach. Because jurisdiction is a matter of ecclesiastical disciplinary law and not divine law, the exercise of jurisdiction has been significantly modified in the 1983 code. Both laymen and -women can share jurisdiction in so far as they "cooperate" with those in orders:

"Those who are in sacred orders are, in accordance with the provisions of law, capable of the power of governance, which belongs to the church by divine institution. This power is also called the power of jurisdiction.

"Lay members of Christ's faithful can cooperate in the exercise of this same power in accordance with the law" (c. 129).

While the new code has not changed the fact that preaching requires a call from Church authority, the law now allows the laity to "cooperate" in the exercise of jurisdiction, and, therefore, the appropriate authority can authorize them to preach in the name of the Church.

THE FACULTY TO PREACH IN THE NEW CODE
Unlike the 1917 code, which required that "mission" to preach always be explicitly given by competent authority, today Canon Law itself gives the faculty to each priest and deacon:

"Without prejudice to the provisions of canon 765,[2] priests and deacons, with at least the presumed consent of the rector of a church, have the faculty to preach everywhere unless this faculty has been restricted or removed by the competent Ordinary, or unless particular law requires express permission" (c. 764).

In spite of the fact that there has been a major shift from the 1917 code, which gave authority to preach only to those with jurisdiction, this does not mean that the faculty to preach is now derived from the power of orders. The faculty to preach is still an effect of jurisdiction, but the law presumes that those in orders will, in fact, exercise an office that will require preaching because the exercise of sacred orders requires the exercise of some dimension of the teaching office.

Since the law itself gives the faculty to preach, the law also presumes the preacher will be qualified to preach. The 1917 code demanded that the authority granting

45

the faculty to preach be certain of the preacher's good morals and doctrinal competence. So strict was this requirement of doctrinal competency that it was to be determined by means of an examination (1917 code, c. 1340). The same canon gave the ordinary or superior the power to revoke the preacher's faculty if he learned that he was not qualified to preach.

Although not explicitly stated, the new code presumes that the preacher possesses good morals, competence in doctrine, and an overall ability to communicate. Before a bishop ordains a candidate for the deaconate or priesthood he must be assured that the person has the qualities needed for effective preaching. These include "sound faith . . . right intention . . . requisite knowledge . . . good reputation and . . . moral probity" (c. 1029).

The new code requires that students for the priesthood and permanent deaconate:

1. Be adequately prepared in homiletics (c. 256)
2. Continue their theological education even after ordination (c. 279)

While that law itself gives the faculty to preach to the ordained, Canon 257, 2 also requires that the preacher understand the language, institutions, social conditions, usages, and customs of the community to which he preaches. He may use his faculty "with the presumed permission of the rectors of churches." The law uses the term "rector" to identify the one in charge including pastors, canonical administrators, and moderators of parochial teams because these persons have the responsibility to see that the word is preached with competence and doctrinal integrity to those in their charge. If they have reason to believe that this will not be done, they can refuse permission to preach.

Canon 772, 1, gives the diocesan bishop the power to make norms for preaching for his diocese. A diocesan bishop can restrict priests or deacons who are incardinated in his diocese from preaching. This restriction can be total or partial, limited to certain places. Furthermore, the bishop can restrict the preaching by clerics from other dioceses or religious institutes who may be in his own diocese. Theoretically, a bishop could enact a policy whereby no ordained cleric can preach in his diocese without specific permission. In such cases, the bishop would have to make this restriction known because, theoretically, an ordained cleric has the faculty to preach anywhere.

THE QUALITY OF PREACHING: CONTENT, DELIVERY, PREPARATION

The very fact that divine law gives the ministry of preaching to the bishops presupposes that they and their priest collaborators possess the knowledge, creativity and originality to satisfy this obligation. This also means that, as the 1983 *Code of Canon Law* affirms, the faithful have a right to a certain quality of delivery and preparation as well as content of what is preached.[3] They have a right to expect that the preacher prepare himself sufficiently to preach. They have a right to more than "canned" sermons, which are no more than repetitions of other preacher's words or similar widely circulated "aids" for the busy priest.

The word of God itself is unchanging; yet, its application to people and the circumstances of their lives varies from place to place, day to day, and culture to culture. Consequently, Church law sees preaching as an active ministry that demands personal dynamism on the part of the Church's ministers. Canon Law expects the preacher to personally study the circumstances of the people to whom he preaches, to personally contemplate the Scriptures, and to personally adapt his message of salvation in a way that will meet the needs of his listeners and move them to respond in faith.

REQUIREMENTS FOR PREACHERS

The law of the Church assumes that the preacher should be able to explain the meaning of a scriptural passage and move his listeners to believe the word of God and to commit themselves to living it. Consequently, the code contains canons that determine the intellectual, moral, and educational backgrounds the official preacher needs to enable him to both understand and communicate the meaning of the Scriptures. By law, therefore, preachers need faith to believe in what they say and to live the gospel they profess.

THE MINISTERS OF PREACHING

Church law makes a distinction between "ordinary" and "extraordinary" ministers. The ordinary minister of any sacrament or ecclesiastical act is the person upon whom falls the right and duty to perform it, usually because of ordination as a sacred minister, installation to a ministry, or possession of an ecclesiastical office. The extraordinary minister is one who is deputed to exercise the ministry by a particular designation of competent authority.

The Ordinary Ministers of Preaching: General Considerations

The ordinary ministers of preaching in the Latin rite are bishops, priests, and deacons. By divine law, bishops possess the right to preach everywhere. The 1983 code gives priests and deacons the faculty to preach everywhere unless this is restricted by their superiors or particular legislation. The extraordinary ministers of preaching are the laity and nonordained religious.

Both the *Decree on Priestly Life and Ministry*, No. 4, of the Second Vatican Council and the *Rite of Ordination* insist that preaching is one of the principal functions of the ordained. In the *Rite of Ordination of a Priest*, the bishop's instruction describes for the people what the new priest will be:

"By consecration he will be made a true priest of the new Testament, to preach the Gospel, sustain God's people, and celebrate the liturgy, above all the Lord's sacrifice."[4]

During the ordination ceremony, the bishop asks the candidate to make four declarations to the assembled community regarding his intentions to undertake the priestly office. One of these declarations is an affirmative response to the question posed by the bishop:

"Are you resolved to exercise the ministry of the Word worthily and wisely, preaching the Gospel and explaining the Catholic faith?"[5]

Similarly, in the *Rite of Ordination of a Deacon*, the bishop addresses the candidate concerning his role to "not only listen to God's Word but also to preach it."[6]

Because candidates for ordination must undergo a lengthy period of preparation, which concentrates on the study of the various areas of theology and the Sacred Scriptures as well as a constant program of spiritual formation, Church law has always presumed that a cleric, once he is ordained, possesses the requisite qualities to preach. For this reason, those in sacred orders are the ordinary ministers of preaching.

Practically speaking, the priests are responsible for most of the preaching in our churches and chapels. As special cooperators of the bishops, the priests represent the Church on the local level and are most instrumental in the formation of the faithful. It is not surprising, then, that priests are singled out in Canon 762:

"The people of God are first united through the word of the living God, and are fully entitled to seek this word from their priests. For this reason, sacred ministers are to consider the office of preaching as of great importance, since proclaiming the Gospel of God to all is among their principal duties."

Simply put, the faithful have a right to expect that all priests, whether parish priests or not, have as their foremost duty the preaching of God's word. Because bishops enjoy the fullness of the priesthood, they can be expected to be especially zealous in carrying out this duty.

Deacons
Canon 762 also uses the term "sacred ministers" in connection with preaching. This legal term includes deacons as well as bishops and priests. With ordination to the deaconate, the first of the sacred orders, a man becomes a cleric and assumes the consequent obligations. Thus, the deacon shares in the responsibility and obligation to preach. His responsibility is learning to preach, preparing to preach and being able to preach a message that may bring his listeners to do God's will.

THE OFFICES OF PREACHING
We have thus far considered the mandate to preach and its relationship to ordination. There are two offices in the Church that impose a grave obligation to preach. These are the office of ordinary (residential bishop) and the office of pastor. Pastors are priests who assist the ordinary by assuming the care over particular portions of the local Church (parishes).

Bishops
By divine law, the bishops, as successors to the Apostles, have the primary obligation in the Church of

Christ to preach the gospel. Canon Law requires that they themselves preach and see that those who assist them also fulfill the law:

"The diocesan bishop is bound to teach and illustrate to the faithful the truths of faith which are to be believed and applied to behaviour. He is himself to preach frequently. He is also to ensure that the provisions of the canons on the ministry of the word, especially on the homily and catechetical instruction, are faithfully observed, so that the whole of Christian teaching is transmitted to all" (c. 386, 1).

According to the legal interpretations of this canon, the bishop himself should preach frequently, not only in his cathedral, but throughout his diocese. By so doing, he gives both an example and an encouragement to the priests who will see his action as an example of the importance of preaching. Secondly, in his ongoing care for parish life, the 1983 code reminds the bishop that he must make sure that the priests and others properly respond to their preaching obligations. Needless to say, he is not only to make sure that preaching is done, but that it is done effectively. To this end, the bishop is responsible for providing continuing education for his clergy.

Pastors

Perhaps the single most influential office in the Church is that of pastor. While the canons and many theological documents often mean bishops when they refer to "sacred pastors," the term more commonly refers to those priests who are given the charge of leadership in a parish, a community of the faithful entrusted to a pastor (c. 515, 1).

The pastor has direct, day-to-day contact with the faithful, preaching, presiding over the eucharistic liturgies and celebrating the sacraments of the Church with his faithful people. As a result, the parish is the place where the vast majority of Catholics come to know the Lord through the teaching of their pastor and his associates in ministry. Therefore, Canon Law legislates:

"The parish priest [pastor] has the obligation of ensuring that the word of God is proclaimed in its entirety to those living in the parish. He is therefore to see to it that the lay members of Christ's faithful are instructed in the truths of faith, especially by means of the homily on Sundays and holy days of obligation and by catechetical formation" (c. 528, 1).

The pastor's duty to preach is emphasized by legislation found in both the 1917 and the 1983 codes, which reserves certain parochial functions to pastors. As leader of the parish, he has the right and duty to preside at the more important ecclesiastical functions involving his parishioners where he will have a special opportunity to preach.

For this reason, the revised rituals of the sacraments call for a homily whenever the sacrament is celebrated and the law expects pastors to pay special attention to these events and not simply go through the ritual. The *Constitution on the Sacred Liturgy* says:

"Pastors of souls must realize that, when the liturgy is celebrated, more is required than the mere observance of laws governing valid and licit celebration. It is their duty also to ensure that the faithful take part knowingly, actively, and fruitfully" (No. 11).

Canon 530 points out the pastor's right to conduct certain sacramental and ceremonial functions and his obligation to respond adequately to the rights of the faithful to hear the word of God.

Reading this canon in the total context of the code, one can arrive at no conclusion other than it imposes on pastors a grave obligation to preach the word of God personally, or, at least, to see to it that the word is preached, at those vitally important sacramental moments in the life of the parish: birth, marriage and death, the weekly commemoration of the Lord's Resurrection, and the Holy Days of obligation.

Deacons

While deacons are ordinary ministers of preaching, Canon Law does not stress their obligation to preach because it does not consider preaching to be a primary function of the deacon. Rather, other forms of service to the Church are more closely related to the deaconate. McVann's brief treatment of preaching by deacons, based on historical data, clarifies the deacon's right and duty to preach:

"Legislation of recent centuries has made the position of deacons in respect to preaching clear: they are ordinary subjects for preaching faculties. This was not always so. . . . Deacons in the first six centuries exercised the office reciting aloud the Sacred Scriptures, and the verb *praedicare* is used to describe that act; from time to time they also read aloud the homilies of the fathers when the bishop or priest was hindered from preaching. True, deacons of the period had a large share in the instruction of catechumens. And we find instances where a deacon of high ability would be admitted to public preaching at the bidding of his bishop. Yet it does not seem that preaching, as we understand the term, was for a long time regarded as an ordinary part of the deacon's office."[7]

Although deacons theoretically enjoyed the right to preach before the restoration of the permanent deaconate in 1964, their preaching was exercised mostly in the seminary setting and for the most part consisted of practice sermons. Seldom did they preach in parish churches because the seminarians' time in the deaconate was usually limited to several months or a year prior to priestly ordination.

Vatican II called for the restoration of the permanent deaconate in both the Latin and Oriental churches. For the Latin Church, this mandate took practical effect with the issue of the Papal Decree (*motu proprio*), *Sacrum diaconatus ordinem* on June 18, 1967. Preaching is mentioned there in two places:

"In addition, there should be familiarity and practice . . . in giving talks and exhortations to the people. . . ."

This excerpt pertains to the training of permanent deacons and its relationship to their regular duties. The second reference is found among the listed functions of the deacon:

"to read the Scriptures to the faithful and to teach and preach to the people."

The deacon is always an ordinary minister of preaching. Canon Law gives to him, as to the priest, the faculty to preach. Nevertheless, diocesan or parish policy is quite likely to restrict the use of this faculty by both permanent deacons and deacons who are training to be priests to ensure that deacons receive adequate doctrinal preparation as well as preparation in the art of preaching itself. In a number of dioceses, for instance, permanent deacons are specially examined for the preaching ministry before they are given permission to preach.

Most deacons exercise their ministry in parochial settings or as associate chaplains. Transient deacons destined for the priesthood are required, in many seminaries or dioceses, to spend several months to a year completing an internship period in a parish in which they exercise a supervised ministry. A vitally important part of this is preaching on a regular basis with planned critiques and guidance.

Opportunities for deaconal preaching are many and varied: they may preach at funeral services, benedictions of the Blessed Sacrament, weddings, communion services, penance services or other liturgical or paraliturgical gatherings. The deacon can also preach at the Eucharist by giving the homily. A problem arises, however, in that the liturgical norms urge that "the homily should ordinarily be given by the celebrant."[8]

Since a deacon is never the celebrant at the Eucharist, how can this liturgical regulation be reconciled with his general ministry to preach?

In the first place, the liturgical law cited above does not mandate that the celebrant always deliver the homily. While this is certainly more correct in the liturgical sense, there may be occasions when it would be more fitting and even effective for the deacon to preach than the celebrant.

Because preaching the homily is not a primary duty of the deacon, he need not preach whenever he assists at the Eucharist. Preaching the homily by the deacon can and may take place at the Eucharist, but this should be suited to the particular needs of the congregation, the event, and the deacon's capabilities.

As to the Sunday Eucharist, both the canons and the liturgical law seem to indicate that the priest-celebrant of the Eucharist should also deliver the homily. When transient or permanent deacons do so, it should be by way of exception and not a regular practice.

EXTRAORDINARY MINISTERS OF PREACHING
As previously explained, Canon Law establishes two categories of ministers: ordinary and extraordinary. In

some cases, the nature of the action determines who can be either an ordinary or extraordinary minister. For example, the ordinary minister for the distribution of Holy Communion is the bishop, priest, or deacon; yet, under certain circumstances bishops depute lay persons to be extraordinary ministers of the Eucharist—the eucharistic ministers so frequently encountered at Sunday Masses in recent times. Such deputation is possible because ordination is not required to give the consecrated Eucharist to a person.

On the other hand, the only minister of the sacrament of reconciliation is a priest (and implicitly of course, a bishop). There can be no extraordinary minister of reconciliation because the holy order of priesthood is required for the valid celebration of this sacrament.

For the various reasons cited, bishops, priests, and deacons are the ordinary ministers of preaching. Anyone else who preaches in the name of the Church is an extraordinary minister who takes the place of the ordinary minister and performs some or all of his duties by reason of deputation by legitimate authority.

Conscious of its mission to proclaim Christ in all his truth, the Church seeks to guarantee, as far as possible, that the word of God preached in the name of the Church is both authentic and Spirit-filled. Just as the Church legislates extensive requirements for the ordinary minister, so also the Church also sets requirements for the extraordinary minister of preaching.

In the broadest sense, all baptized Christians share in and support the ministry of preaching in so far as their lives cause others to see in them a commitment to the Lord. This is clear from Canon 759 of the 1983 code:

"The lay members of Christ's faithful, by reason of their baptism and confirmation, are witnesses to the good news of the Gospel, by their words and by the examples of their Christian life. They can also be called upon to cooperate with Bishops and priests in the exercise of the ministry of the word."

This canon recognizes that being a Christian demands continual conversion. The good examples of those whose faith empowers them to live up to the demands of the gospel in a special way greatly helps the ongoing conversion of all—believers and nonbelievers alike. When the lives of such persons are seen as authentic expressions of living faith, they can and often do have a more profound effect than the prepared words of the official preachers. All Christians, ordained or not, are called to give this kind of witness.

Preaching is witness in a more restricted sense; it is a specific kind of verbal witness. Because preaching is at the very foundation of the Church and its mission, the Church's ordained ministers are particularly responsible for its proper execution. At the same time, the laity are expected to "cooperate" in this ministry when the needs of the ministry demand it.

This responsibility for preaching is detailed by Church law under what the code calls "care of souls." Only bishops and priests are burdened with this grave responsibility; they alone have the responsibility of being "pastors." The reason for this is because the office of pastor is one of lasting commitment. Customarily, therefore, dioceses assign pastors to serve in parishes for considerable periods of time: five years, eight years, twelve years, or even for life, which is the usual term for the bishop of a diocese.

During these long years, the pastor is required to preach day after day, week after week, year after year, whether he feels like it or not. In fact, Canon Law is really saying to the pastor: "It is your calling by God which you neglect at your peril." As St. Paul said: "Woe unto me, unless I preach the Gospel" (cf. 1 Cor 9:16).

There is no doubt that a qualified lay person may be able to preach a better sermon than his pastor—occasionally. It is highly unlikely, however, given the legitimate demands of lay life, that a layman or -woman could do it on a regular and continuing basis. For one thing, formal preaching is not the lay vocation. Rather, God has chosen to preach his word on a regular, sustaining basis, through the men he has chosen to be pastors.

Nevertheless, the Church recognizes that lay persons can truly preach, if not on a regular, sustained basis, at least from time to time. Consequently, the Church provides for the occasional preaching by the laity as extraordinary ministers of preaching. In this way, they exercise the grace proper to them as cooperators in the care of souls.

The Second Vatican Council reemphasized the fact that not only the clergy but all of the faithful share in the prophetic office of Christ.[9] The laity share in the apostolate of building up the body of Christ in the world:

"The laity, however, are given this special vocation: to make the Church present and fruitful in those places and circumstances where it is only through them that she can become the salt of the earth. . . . Besides this apostolate which belongs to absolutely every Christian, the laity can be called in different ways to more immediate cooperation in the apostolate of the hierarchy. . . . They have, moreover, the capacity of being appointed by the hierarchy to some ecclesiastical offices with a view to a spiritual end" (*Lumen Gentium*, No. 33).

This essential theological understanding of the vocation of the laity is well grounded in *Lumen Gentium's* ecclesiology of the Church as the "People of God." The Church has received a mission of "proclaiming and establishing among all peoples the kingdom of Christ and of God,"[10] which is carried out by the celebration of the sacraments and by the preaching of the word of God. The authorization or mandate to preach, comes from the Church herself.

The 1983 *Code of Canon Law* implements this conciliar teaching in the ordinary life of the Church by recognizing the capacity of lay persons to be extraordinary ministers of preaching and, in the exercise of that ministry, share their gifts with the gathering of the People of God:

"The laity may be allowed to preach in a church or oratory if, in certain circumstances, it is necessary, or, in particular cases, it would be advantageous, according to the provisions of the Episcopal Conference . . ." (c. 766).

The episcopal conferences are to draw up guidelines for the practical application of this canon to a given country. The Church prefers to have national guidelines in order to prevent the vitally important ministry of preaching from deteriorating as a result of haphazard or inconsistent application of the canon.

In particular, episcopal conferences are expected by the Church's law to establish minimum standards of preparation for lay preachers in Scripture, dogma and moral theology, Church law, and history. Nevertheless, even in the absence of such guidelines, individual bishops may and do depute lay persons to preach on special occasions.

Lay Preaching Mentioned in the Liturgical Norms
The liturgical norms mandate three liturgical services
wherein laymen or -women can licitly preach. The first
of these involves services of the Word, celebrated in
place of the Mass when a priest is not available. The
instruction of the Congregation of Rites, "Inter
Oecumenici," on the orderly implementation of the
Constitution on the Sacred Liturgy, describes a service of
the Word with epistle and gospel that can be used outside of the eucharistic liturgy, but is, nonetheless, celebrated in a manner similar to when it is celebrated at
Mass:

"If the one presiding is a deacon, he shall give a homily; a non-deacon shall read a homily chosen by the
bishop or the pastor."[11]

Strictly speaking, of course, the lay person is not giving the homily in such celebrations. Rather, he or she
is reading one composed by someone else just as the
deacons did in the early Church, and which was considered to be preaching.

The ritual for the celebration of baptism by a catechist
when no priest or deacon is available encourages the
catechist to preach. Number 37 of the Instruction says:
"After the reading, the catechist may give a brief homily in the way determined by the bishop."[12]

Finally, the *Directory for Masses with Children* recognizes
that a lay person may be better at preaching to children than a priest:

"With the consent of the pastor or rector of the
church, one of the adults may speak to the children
after the gospel, especially if the priest finds it difficult
to adapt himself to the mentality of the children."[13]

There are further instances where the Church recognizes the unique gifts of lay persons as extraordinary

ministers of preaching. Laymen who are installed in the ministry of lector have as one of their duties the instruction of the faithful on the worthy reception of the sacraments.[14]

Catechists are an important part of the Revised Rite of Christian Initiation of Adults. Number 48 of the norms for that Rite state:

"The office of catechist is important for the progress of the catechumens and for the growth of the community. . . . When they are teaching, they should see that their instruction is filled with the spirit of the Gospel, adapted to the liturgical signs and course of the year."

A lay person may also be an extraordinary minister of preaching during retreats or missions.

Lay Preaching of the Eucharistic Homily: A Particular Question
Canon Law as promulgated in both the 1917 and 1983 codes is emphatic that the homily in the eucharistic liturgy is to be preached only by ordained clergy. Moreover, lay persons may not preach the homily in any of the sacramental liturgies except when the liturgical books explicitly allow it, as at baptismal services performed by catechists.

When the Second Vatican Council sought to bring about a renewal of preaching, it emphasized the renewal of the eucharistic homily. After the conclusion of the Council, many inquiries were submitted to some of the pertinent Vatican Congregations about the appropriateness of lay persons preaching the homily. The Pontifical Commission for the Interpretation of the Decrees of the Second Vatican Council gave the authoritative reply to these questions in its response of January 11, 1971. The pertinent texts follow:

"Whether the words 'the homily should ordinarily be given by the celebrant himself,' by which the prescriptions of the Constitution *Sacrosanctum Concilium*, n. 52 and the Dogmatic Constitution *Dei Verbum*, n. 24 are made effective . . . must be so interpreted that those who are neither priests nor deacons but are men and women, who, however, participate in the sacred liturgy, can give the homily?

"Reply. In the negative."[15]

Yet, for all the reasonable legislation of the Church, so in conformity to biblical teaching and born out of painful experiences of heretical preaching over the centuries, the question remains: What about those lay people who feel a compelling inner call to preach and who would be manifestly competent at it? Cannot an exception be made for them?

It is clear that while an inner call and native talent coupled with theological knowledge and faith are necessary for preaching, these do not yet complete the requirements for preaching the homily. In fact, while these may be sufficient for deputation to other forms of preaching, as Canon 767 says, the eucharistic homily is the Church of Christ's "most important" form of preaching.

When we carefully reflect on the history of the Church, the abuse of preaching, which has often resulted in serious error, and when we consider the unique sacredness of the Holy Sacrifice of the Mass, the Church's exacting regulation of the ministry of preaching makes perfect sense.

There are different ways of preaching just as there are different ways of witnessing, and Canon Law does not give the clergy a monopoly on the word of God. Lay persons are asked by the Church to preach in a variety of ways today. The single exception is the eucharistic homily. It is so intimately related to the sacramental presence of Christ that it is ordinarily to be preached by the celebrant and occasionally by another cleric. But, in all cases, the eucharistic homily is the special provenance of the ordained.

NOTES

1. Cf. Canon 756, 1. *The Code of Canon Law in English Translation* (London: Collins Liturgical Publications, 1983).

2. Canon 765 says: To preach to religious in their churches or oratories, permission is required of the Superior who is competent according to the constitutions of the religious community.

3. Cf. Canons 760 and 528.

4 *The Rites of the Catholic Church* (New York: Pueblo Press, 1940), Vol II, p. 62.

5. Ibid., p. 64.

6. Ibid., p. 52.

7. James McVann, *The Canon Law on Sermon Preaching* (New York: Paulist Press, 1940).

8. *General Instruction on the Roman Missal*, n. 42.

9. *Lumen Gentium*, No. 12.

10. *Lumen Gentium*, No. 5.

11. In *Documents on the Liturgy: 1963–1979* (Collegeville, MN: Liturgical Press, 1982), p. 95.

12. *Rites of the Catholic Church* (New York: Pueblo Publishing Co., 1976), Vol. 1, n. 137, p. 240

13. In *Documents on the Liturgy*, op. cit., p. 682.

14. *Ministeria quaedam*, No. 4.

15. *Canon Law Digest*, ed. by James O'Conner, S.J. (Chicago: The Chicago Province of the Society of Jesus), Vol. 7, p. 633. The *Instruction on the Roman Missal* states that the celebrant

of the Mass "should" preach the homily; it did not say he "must" preach it. The inquiry was based on the question whether or not the use of the words "should" and "ordinarily" in the Instruction excluded nonclerics, or whether it left room for them to give the homily by way of exception. The response says that lay persons cannot give the homily even by way of exception.

Subsequently, in response to a petition submitted by the president of the German Bishops' Conference, the Congregation for the Clergy issued a decree[1] permitting the German bishops to grant the faculty to preach to qualified and worthy lay persons. This permission lasted for a four-year period. In the dispositive section of the decree, the theological basis for restricting preaching at liturgical services (especially the homily) to sacred ministers is summarized. The decree then states that due to the special circumstances of the German dioceses, particularly the shortage of priests, the right of the faithful to the word of God justified an exception to the general rule of law.

In those places where priests and deacons were lacking, the bishops were permitted to give a canonical mission to lay persons capable of preaching the homily at non-eucharistic celebrations of the word of God. In fact, the bishops could depute lay persons to preach the homily even if it were only a matter of the celebrant of the Mass being physically or morally impeded from discharging his office. Finally, the bishops could authorize the use of an extraordinary minister if special circumstances or celebrations warranted a homily by a well-qualified lay person. One point was very clear, however, the dispensation underscored the law that laicized priests are forbidden to preach under any circumstances.

Interestingly enough, upon its expiration, this indult was not renewed. It had been reported that lay persons were, in fact, becoming recognized as ordinary ministers of preaching in situations where there were sufficient numbers of priests.

Later, in 1984, the German Bishops' Conference again submitted a request to the Holy See, asking that lay persons be allowed to deliver the homily when the priest was morally or physically unable to do so. Their request was refused and the response, dated Feb. 22, 1985, stated quite clearly that the priest-celebrant was to give the homily.[2]

The restriction of the homily to ordained ministers conforms to the historical development of this special medium of preaching. It also conforms to liturgical legislation and practice, which holds that the eucharistic homily should ordinarily be given by the celebrant.

1. S. C. Clergy, Nov. 20, 1973, private reply, in *Canon Law Digest*, Vol. 8, pp. 941–944.
2. S. C. Clergy, Letter to Cardinal Hoeffner, private, February 22, 1985, unpublished.

Chapter Three

The Goal of Preaching: Building Christian Community

CURRENT PRACTICE: PRIVATE SPIRITUALITY
The goal of much preaching today is the nourishment of the faith life of the Christian as an individual. Such preaching encourages the Christian to read his Bible, say his prayers, receive the sacraments, practice personal discipline, grow in the moral virtues, take up his cross, and become a saint.

There is something very private about the spirituality this kind of preaching leads to. The individual can fulfill all its requirements for holiness for the most part alone and apart from others. He meditates alone; he prays alone; he suffers in silence and alone.

Granted that baptism, confirmation, ordination, and marriage are always community affairs, they are also once-in-a-lifetime events for a Christian. The sacraments that we repeat, sometimes frequently, on the other hand, can be quite private affairs. The sacrament of the anointing can be received in a hospital room or at home alone. The individual makes a private confession alone.

The only sacrament that demands a community for religious experience on a regular basis is the Eucharist. And even here people frequently go to Mass only as individuals, more to receive Holy Communion than to hear the word of God and celebrate faith with a believing community. They remain individuals apart, seated separated from one another throughout the Church, sometimes not even exchanging the greeting of peace. This individualistic emphasis is particularly apparent in daily eucharistic celebrations that are offered without music, without preaching, by a small congregation in a large church.

The preaching that encourages this private kind of spirituality is very much in harmony with the American cultural view that religion is a strictly personal matter between the individual and "his" God. It emphasizes the vertical as opposed to the horizontal aspects of the gospel message; it stresses love of God more than love of neighbor. Consequently, this God-oriented preaching can be very comforting and comfortable, both for the preacher and for his congregation, because it does not require any real public witness or involvement with one's neighbor or his needs.

There is no doubt that preaching the social aspects of the gospel provokes controversy. Christians do not agree as to what specific stands should be taken on specific issues in the public forum, or even, at times, what principles should govern the exploration of the issues. Yet explore them they must. Pope John XXIII wrote:

"Here once more We exhort Our Sons to take an active part in public life, and to work together for the benefit of the whole human race, as well as for that of their own political communities" (*Peace on Earth*, No. 146).[1]

Wanting to help the faithful of the United States fulfill this duty, the bishops of the United States issued a Pastoral Letter, *The Challenge of Peace: God's Promise and Our Response*, to apply the moral teaching of the Church to the specific issues of our day. At the same time, they recognized vast differences in interpretation and called for charity:

"The experience of preparing this letter has manifested to us the range of strongly held opinion in the Catholic community on questions of both fact and judgment concerning issues of war and peace. We urge mutual respect among individuals and groups in the church as this letter is analyzed and discussed. Obviously, as bishops, we believe that such differences should be expressed within the framework of Catholic moral teaching. We need in the church not only conviction and commitment, but also civility and charity."

The disagreement among the faithful, sometimes very intense, has caused many preachers to avoid significant preaching about the social consequences of the gospel for the larger community. Instead, they emphasize personal devotion and spirituality, personal and family virtue, liturgical and private prayer.

THE GOAL OF PREACHING: SOCIAL TRANSFORMATION

Although this pastoral attitude is thoroughly understandable, nevertheless, the goal of Christian preaching is not simply personal, individual reform. In spite of the plethora of problems inherent in achieving it, the goal of Christian preaching is ultimately social transformation. *The Pastoral Constitution on the Church* says:

"Profound and rapid changes make it particularly urgent that no one, ignoring the trend of events or drugged by laziness, content himself with a merely individualistic morality. It grows increasingly true that the obligations of justice and love are fulfilled only if each person, contributing to the common good, according to his own abilities and the needs of others, also promotes and assists the public and private institutions dedicated to bettering the conditions of human life" (No. 30).

Pope Paul VI specified in greater detail how preaching the gospel betters the conditions of human life:

"For the Church it is a question not only of preaching the Gospel in ever wider geographic areas or to ever greater numbers of people, but also of affecting and as it were upsetting, through the power of the Gospel, mankind's criteria of judgment, determining values, points of interest, lines of thought, sources of inspiration and models of life, which are in contrast with the word of God and the plan of salvation" (*Apostolic Exhortation on Evangelization in the Modern World*, No. 19).

Human Solidarity
The gospel unmistakably teaches that none of us can be saved alone, in a vacuum apart from one another. Our eternal destiny depends on our treatment of others. Jesus said:

"Come, you who are blessed by my Father. Inherit the kingdom prepared for you from the foundation of the world. For I was hungry and you gave me food, I was thirsty and you gave me drink, a stranger and you welcomed me, naked and you clothed me, ill and you cared for me, in prison and you visited me" (Mt 25:34–36).

All Christian preaching, therefore, is done for the purpose of building of Christian community so that the community can spread the gospel to "the ends of the earth." Because the experience of community is inherent in the social nature of human beings, community has been a significant factor in the communication of divine revelation.

In recent years, the rise of the nuclear family, the development of a highly mobile society, and the adop-

tion of a life-style increasingly geared to single-living
has lessened our sensitivity to community. At the
same time the experience of community is lessening,
the hunger for it is increasing.

Prior to Vatican II, the Church defined itself as the
"perfect society," meaning that it possessed all those
things needed to lead believers to salvation. This short
definition, while still true, does not communicate the
full nature of the Church as concisely as the Second
Vatican Council's teaching that the Church is the "People of God." The Council more accurately sums up the
teaching of Scripture by replacing the notion of the
Church's being a perfect society, which served so well
during one period of the Church's life, with the understanding that the Church is the pilgrim people on
their way through history in hope of meeting the Father. In so doing, it gives clear expression to the reality of Christian solidarity throughout the entire world:

"Among all the nations of earth there is but one People of God, which takes its citizens from every race,
making them citizens of a kingdom which is a heavenly and not an earthly nature. For all the faithful scat-
tered throughout the world are in communion with
each other in the Holy Spirit" (*Dogmatic Constitution on
the Church*, No. 13).

The *Code of Canon Law* draws on the riches of the *Dogmatic Constitution on the Church* and makes clear how
the faithful are incorporated into Christ: they are constituted the people of God through baptism. For the
first time Church law, responding to an obvious
need in an age of pluralism, defines the bonds of
membership.

"Those baptized are in full communion with the Catholic Church here on earth who are joined with Christ in
his visible body, through the bonds of *profession of*

faith, the sacraments and *ecclesiastical governance"* (c. 205, italics added).

Canon 204 reflects the conciliar teaching that the Church of the Spirit, the charismatic Church, is one and the same with the structured Church:

"This Church, established and ordered in this world as a society, subsists in the Catholic Church, governed by the successor of Peter and the bishops in communion with him" (c. 204, 2).

The members of the Christian community do not constitute a merely passive people. Church law says that each member of the Church participates in his own way in the priestly, prophetic, and kingly office of Christ. In other words, all are called "to exercise the mission which God entrusted to his people to fulfill in the world" (c. 204, 1).

The work of the preacher, fundamentally grounded in the "mission which is entrusted to the Church," is directly related to the three aspects of bonding to the Church. First, the profession of faith contains the basic elements of the preacher's message. Next, the sacraments are occasions for teaching the meaning of Christ in the lives of the faithful as well as moments when faith itself is nourished. Finally, ecclesiastical governance provides a structure that can even be seen as a vehicle for spreading the word in the world.

The preaching and teaching of the Church flow from the obligation of mission, which all believers share.

"All Christ's faithful have the obligation and the right to strive so that the divine message of salvation may more and more reach all people of all times and places" (c. 211).

Because the obligation to participate in mission is grounded in baptism and confirmation (c. 225, 1), all members of the Church have an equal duty to promote apostolic action "according to their state and condition" (cf. c. 216). Consequently, mission is not limited to the hierarchy, clergy, and religious; quite the opposite, the spreading of the gospel is basic to all Christians.

It follows, as a matter of course, that those who are called to spread the Christian message must also be nourished by that same message. Canon Law expresses the need for nourishment in terms both of rights and obligations.

The Rights of the Faithful

The law of the Church protects the believing community by guiding those fallible and frail human beings who are in leadership positions. The leaders' first responsibility, as would be expected, is toward the nourishment of the Church itself.

"Christ's faithful have the right to be assisted by their Pastors from the spiritual riches of the Church, especially by the word of God and the sacraments" (c. 213).

Because the faithful have been called to lead a holy life and to proclaim Christ's message, the right to education is fundamental (cf. c. 217).

The right to proper formation and education is reaffirmed in Canon 229 in a more specific manner. Reiterating the fact that people have to know the message of Christ in order to live it, the canon states:

"Lay people have the duty and the right to acquire the knowledge of Christian teaching which is appropriate to each's capacity and condition, so that they may be able to live according to this teaching, to proclaim it and if necessary, to defend it, and may be capable of playing their part in the exercise of the apostolate" (c. 229).

In this canon, the essential right to education in the Christian message is grounded in the obligation to mission.

The law, then, sees preaching as an activity that is directed outward to the faithful. Preaching is not a personal possession of the minister. If there are restrictions on who can preach, what can be preached, and the like, they are there for the good of the faithful.

Preparing Seminarians To Preach
Although divine law mandates the bishops to preach, priests and deacons participate in this mandate. In fact, most people hear the word of God explained to them not by their bishop, but by their parish priests, chaplains, and others. Furthermore, all bishops are priests before their elevation to the episcopacy, and one of the essential criteria for choosing a bishop is his ability and willingness to preach the Word. It is not surprising, then, that Canon Law lays down certain important requirements for the formation of seminarians to prepare them to preach the word of God effectively.

First of all, they are to be trained to be able to make the timeless word of the Lord real by relating it to the questions and problems of their age. Consequently, Canon 248 requires that students destined for the priesthood receive a solid grounding in the "sacred sciences together with a general culture which is appropriate to the needs of place and time" (c. 248).

While faith is the basis of preaching, this intellectual training enables the preacher to fulfill the mandate of the canon:

"[Future priests] ought to be able properly to proclaim the Gospel to the people of their own time, in a fashion suited to the manner of the people's thinking" (c. 248).

This canon does not mean that future priests are to be taught to accommodate the gospel to popular fads. It does not mean that preachers are to modify the gospel message to suit the passing needs or whims of society. Were this so, preachers could merely entertain their audiences and reduce the message of Scripture to harmless platitudes.

Actually, Canon 248 levies an onerous charge on those who are responsible for priestly formation. They are to see to it that the seminarians are adequately prepared to travel the rough road of uncovering the meaning of the Scriptures as intended by the Lord and proclaimed by the sacred writers. This point is further emphasized with Canon 252, which stipulates that theological formation is to take place "in the light of faith and under the guidance of the magisterium."

This emphasis by Canon Law on the centrality of preaching and the sacraments in priestly ministry is based on the revealed truth that the Eucharist and the other sacraments are real encounters with Christ and the center around which the Church exists. Through the sacraments, Christ becomes present to us, nourishes us, and guides us as we build up his Body, the Church. The Second Vatican Council tells us:

"The purpose of the sacraments is to sanctify men, to build up the Body of Christ, and finally, to give worship to God. Because they are signs they also instruct" (*Constitution on the Sacred Liturgy*, No. 59).

Continuing Formation in Preaching
Preparation to preach effectively does not end with the end of seminary formation. Canon 279 mandates

the ongoing education of priests to ensure that they continue to be equipped to preach and teach in a manner suitable to God's word:

"Clerics are to continue their sacred studies even after ordination to the priesthood. They are to hold to that solid doctrine based on Sacred Scripture which has been handed down by our forebears and which is generally received by the Church, as set out especially in the documents of the Councils and the Roman Pontiffs. They are to avoid profane novelties and pseudo-science" (c. 279, 1).

This canonical reminder is well-grounded in a realistic need for today's Church. Sacred ministers are constantly confronted with a rapidly developing society that raises new and difficult questions about the meaning of the gospel message and its demands. Like any other professional, the priest must keep up with developments in his field or his effectiveness will quickly diminish.

"Pop" theology, simplistic comic-strip commentaries, watered down cliches, and childish stories are not adequate to overcome the difficult challenges posed by a rapidly advancing and multifaceted technology that seeks to redefine so many aspects of our society. On the contrary, the preacher must digest a flood of rather sophisticated information in order to begin to comprehend the way to apply the gospel to our world.

It is for reasons such as these that the canons dealing with the obligations and rights of clerics include several that speak to the cleric's manner of life. These canons are related to the duty of preaching because the way a cleric lives influences greatly the credibility of his message. A preacher can neutralize even the best prepared and most eloquently delivered sermon if his hearers know that he does not live what he preaches.

The code, therefore, legislates the following basic obligations to assure credibility in preaching: (1) clerics have a special obligation to show reverence and obedience to the Holy Father and to their ordinary [bishop] (c. 273), (2) they have a special obligation to seek holiness in their lives (c. 276), (3) clerics should shun those things that are unbecoming their state (c. 285, 1), and (4) they are to do their utmost to foster peace and harmony among peoples (c. 287).

At one time, negligence in preaching on Sundays and certain feasts was listed among the canonical crimes (1917 code, c. 2382). The bishop could apply penalties, including removing the negligent preacher from the parish. Whereas the canon did not specify exactly what constituted negligence, commentaries indicate that it included both a failure to preach and repeated preaching of very poor quality.

The newly promulgated *Code of Canon Law* not only reminds preachers of their duty to proclaim the word clearly, it specifically appeals to them to fulfill their duty to preach with faith, understanding, and devotion. Canon 747 is an eloquent attestation of the need for sound preaching in today's world:

"It is the obligation and inherent right of the Church, independent of any human authority, to preach the Gospel to all peoples, using for this purpose even its own means of social communication; for it is to the Church that Christ the Lord entrusted the deposit of faith, so that by the assistance of the Holy Spirit, it might conscientiously guard revealed truth, more intimately penetrate it, and faithfully proclaim and expound it" (c. 747).

PREACHING TO BUILD THE LOCAL CHURCH
The goal of preaching in the Church Universal is the building up the Body of Christ and the transformation

of society through the power of the gospel. Thus it follows that in the local Church, the preacher needs to build up a sense of local solidarity in Christ that is expressed in terms of specific activities and values in specific gatherings of real people. Without local solidarity, preaching cannot really bear fruit.

These local gatherings occur first around the preaching of the word of God and the celebration of the liturgy, which is both the source and summit of Christian activity.[2] The worshiping community is endowed with many gifts to be used for the work that Christ calls it to do. St. Paul, for example, wrote about the wide variety of spiritual gifts functioning in the Corinthian community:

"To one is given through the Spirit the expression of wisdom; to another the expression of knowledge according to the same Spirit; to another faith by the same Spirit; to another gifts of healing by the one Spirit; to another mighty deeds; to another prophecy; to another discernment of spirits; to another varieties of tongues; to another interpretation of tongues. But one and the same Spirit produces all of these, distributing them individually to each person as he wishes" (1 Cor 12:8–11).

The Spirit continues to give the Church a wide variety of gifts, of which Paul's list is only a brief sample. These gifts have to be activated in the local Church. For example, the Christian community can work to heal the scars of poverty and sickness that afflict the poor. Some gifts lead to the pastoral care of families torn by dissent and cruelty. Through well-coordinated activities, Christ's presence is manifested first to the local community and then to the world. In such ways, the Church community becomes the salt of the earth and the light of the world.[3]

A Community of Joyful Believers
The Good News is good news because it brings joy to
the hearts of even suffering human beings. Jesus said:

"I have told you this so that my joy might be in you
and your joy might be complete" (Jn 15:11).

Therefore, the first quality the preacher should foster
in his community is a sense of happiness because we
are possessed by Christ and belong to one another. St.
Paul writes to the Philippians:

"Rejoice in the Lord always. I shall say it again: rejoice! Your kindness should be known to all. The Lord
is near. Have no anxiety at all, but in everything, by
prayer and petition, with thanksgiving, make your re-
quests known to God. Then the peace of God that surpasses all understanding will guard your hearts and
minds in Christ Jesus" (Phil 4:4–7).

The Christian community is the gathering of people
who are basically joyful and at peace because they
have experienced the nearness of Christ and the generosity of God; that is, they know who they are and
where they are going. Because they experience being
loved by God as his children, they have a good self-
identity: they are one with Christ for all eternity.

At the same time, of course, the promise of Christ
does not remove all suffering and pain. Even for joy-
ous Christians, life has its very painful moments
caused by suffering, disease, rejection. Nevertheless,
suffering and pain are not the cause of unhappiness.
We can be in intense pain and still experience peace
and joy because we are in union with Christ on his
cross. In fact, Paul argues that Christ sustains us even
in the midst of suffering:

"But we hold this treasure [the knowledge of God's
glory] in earthen vessels, that the surpassing power
may be of God and not from us. We are afflicted in

every way, but not constrained; perplexed, but not driven to despair; persecuted, but not abandoned; struck down, but not destroyed; always carrying about in the body the dying of Jesus, so that the life of Jesus may also be manifested in our body. Therefore we are not discouraged; rather, although our outer self is wasting away, our inner self is being renewed day by day. For this momentary light affliction is producing for us an eternal weight of glory beyond all comparison, as we look not to what is seen but to what is unseen; for what is seen is transitory, but what is unseen is eternal" (2 Cor 4:7–10; 16,17).

The root cause of human unhappiness is not suffering. The root cause of unhappiness is sin, and the root cause of joy is deliverance from sin. Sin alienates us from God, makes us unsure about ourselves, traps us in constant delusion about the nature of the world and human life. Sin leads to frustration, anxiety, and eventually to despair.

St. Paul compares the fruits of sin and the happiness that comes from the Spirit in a significant passage from his letter to the Galatians:

"Now the works of the flesh are obvious: immorality, impurity, licentiousness, idolatry, sorcery, hatreds, rivalry, jealousy, outbursts of fury, acts of selfishness, dissensions, factions, occasions of envy, drinking bouts, orgies, and the like. I warn you, as I warned you before, that those who do such things will not inherit the kingdom of God. In contrast, the fruit of the Spirit is love, joy, peace, patience, kindness, generosity, faithfulness, gentleness, self-control. Against such there is no law. Now those who belong to Christ Jesus have crucified their flesh with its passions and desires" (Gal 5:19–24).

Christians who seek to grow in the Lord, therefore, begin that serious process by separating themselves

from their sins of the past through self-denial and as-
cetic practices. Masters of the spiritual life, like John of
the Cross and St. Theresa, or more recent authors like
Garrigou-Lagrange and Tanqueray, have always urged
self-discipline and the embrace of voluntary suffering,
better known as mortification, as prime requirements
for spiritual progress.

Some of the more extreme spiritual guides seem to put
suffering as the goal of Christian life: suffer here, so
you will be rewarded later. When self-denial is overem-
phasized, it may not be long before the worth of an
act of charity depends on how unpleasant it is to perform. The harder to do, the more meritorious to do it.

The great St. Thomas Aquinas, however, taught that it
was not how difficult a thing is to do that matters, but
how good it is to do it. Thus, although it is good (and
necessary) to love an enemy, it is better to love God
first and a friend for love of God.[4]

Christians grow in love, therefore, not by doing hard
things for their own sake, but by seeing God and his
love in whatever we do. This is especially true when it
comes to following the gospel commands by "taking
up one's cross every day" (cf. Lk 9:23-26) and loving
difficult people. When we are successful in loving this
way, the effect of our loving is always joy.

Thanksgiving
The gift of happiness given by the Father of Lights
fills the new believer with a profound desire—need—
to give thanks for the gift of faith he has received. His
whole life becomes one of joy and praise. Those who
were converted to the Lord as adults know with an
especially vivid awareness that when the Spirit takes
possession the heart cries out: "Praise and thanksgiving to our God. Honor, glory and power for ever and
ever" (cf. Rv 5:13).

Life-long Christians, too, as they grow in the Lord, become increasingly sensitive to the greatness of the gift of faith they have been so freely given, and so they are also moved to give praise and thanks.

Paul had the same need to thank God for his gift of conversion, and when he wrote to the saints in Colossae, he reminded them that they had been given the gift of faith so they might experience peace. In return, they had the duty to give thanks:

"Let the peace of Christ control your hearts, the peace into which you were also called in one body. And be thankful" (Col 3:15).

When we remember Jesus' disappointment when only one out of ten lepers returned to give him thanks, we begin to see why the early Christians so stressed the community's need to give corporate thanks. This early custom has perdured forcefully in the Catholic tradition of obligatory Sunday Mass.

In the Eucharist, Jesus has given us the perfect means by which we can return thanks for what we have received. He has given us the perfect sacrifice of praise and thanksgiving—his own flesh and blood. When we eat the Lord's supper in our eucharistic celebrations, we proclaim his death and resurrection, and from the earliest days of the Church, the communities' eucharistic celebrations have been the apex of our Christian lives of worship.[5]

Today, as fervor in Catholic parishes seems to be diminishing, we need to go back to Scripture and the early traditions of the Church to reaffirm our reasons for worshiping as a community. In Paul's first letter, which has been preserved as the inspired word of God, Paul gave some excellent instructions for community living, which we would do well to follow today. He wrote to the Thessalonians:

"We urge you, brothers, admonish the idle, cheer the fainthearted, support the weak, be patient with all. See that no one returns evil for evil; rather, always seek what is good both for each other and for all. Rejoice always. Pray without ceasing. In all circumstances give thanks, for this is the will of God for you in Christ Jesus" (1 Thes 5:14–18).

The sacramental life of the Church, especially the Eucharist can only be celebrated by a believing community. The ordained celebrants of these liturgies, therefore, have a great responsibility before the Lord to celebrate them in a way that enables God's people to give vent to the joy that is moving them to offer thanks. Celebration by a community calls for more from the ordained clergy than just leading a group of individuals through the motions of a rite. *The Constitution on the Sacred Liturgy* puts it this way:

" . . . in order that the liturgy may be able to produce its full effects, it is necessary that the faithful come to it with proper dispositions, that their minds should be attuned to their voices, and that they should cooperate with divine grace lest they receive it in vain. Pastors of souls must therefore realize that, when the liturgy is celebrated, something more is required than the mere observation of the laws governing valid and licit celebration. It is their duty also to ensure that the faithful take part fully aware of what they are doing, actively engaged in the rite, and enriched by it" (No. 11).

Preaching disposes for effective liturgy by helping the celebrating community to recognize God's gifts to them here and now. The preacher should radiate an awareness of God's involvement in his own life and theirs. He should be able to awaken in them a desire to share what they have been given with others, both within the community and outside it. Jesus says:

"Give and gifts will be given to you; a good measure, packed together, shaken down, and overflowing, will be poured into your lap. For the measure with which you measure will in return be measured out to you" (Lk 6:38).

Because money is a constant need in everyday life, and its proper use is a major factor in Christian living, the giving of alms is an important way of thanking God. Paul gives one of his major teachings on thanking God when he takes up a collection of alms for the poor Church in Jerusalem:

"The administration of this public service is not only supplying the needs of the holy ones but is also overflowing in many acts of thanksgiving to God" (2 Cor 9:12).

Hunger for Spiritual and Intellectual Growth
When a person has experienced the grace of God in his life, and when he has entered into a believing community of joy, there is a God-given hunger for greater involvement in the mystery that the community is and celebrates. Consequently, a major thrust of all preaching, but especially parish preaching, should be to motivate Christians to grow in their understanding and appreciation of the word of God. Two examples can illustrate the problem of a lack of spiritual and intellectual growth in Catholic communities that contemporary preaching should vigorously address.

In many dioceses and parishes, religious education programs for youth are neither attracting new students nor holding on to the present ones. Whereas the Church has succeeded in producing the most "professionally trained" catechists it has probably ever had, the Church is attracting fewer children than ever to its programs. Between 1965 and 1985, according to the *Official Catholic Directory*, there was a decline of 31 percent in the number of children under Catholic instruction.

A diocesan director of religious education confided that his program was reaching only 3 percent of the children it should. The situation, however, was even worse than that statistic indicated because he said that 75 percent of those attending the program dropped out before the program was completed.

In many places, adults are not studying their religion either. Large numbers of Catholics stopped studying their religion when they graduated from Catholic school or religion classes. Evidently they were not stimulated there to continue their study of their faith. Publishing statistics show that in general Catholics do not read serious theological works, popular Catholic periodicals, or even diocesan newspapers. Even if nothing else can reach them, adult Bible study should be an integral part of Catholic community life, fostered by exciting biblical preaching.

The Dogmatic Constitution on Divine Revelation stresses the importance of growth in the word of God:

"Just as the life of the Church grows through persistent participation in the eucharistic mystery, so we may hope for a new surge of spiritual vitality from intensified veneration for God's word, which 'lasts forever' " (No. 26).

We will have more to say about spiritual as well as intellectual growth in Chapter Seven on Catechesis.

Moral Goodness: Sign of God's Grace
A good moral life is the inevitable consequence of entrance into the holy people of God. The greatness of God's gifts to his people is revealed through lives of love, self-control, and generosity. In the Gospel according to Matthew, speaking to his disciples, Jesus says:

"You are the light of the world. A city set on a mountain cannot be hidden. Nor do they light a lamp and then put it under a bushel basket; it is set on a lampstand, where it gives light to all in the house. Just so, your light must shine before others, that they may see your good deeds and glorify your heavenly Father" (Mt 5:14–16).

This does not happen only through individual witness. God's love is also revealed through the collective witness of a believing community. Paul commends the Church at Thessalonica for the example of Christianity they offer to the entire world.[6] And in the Gospel of John, Jesus himself stresses the importance of communal witness when he says:

"This is how all will know that you are my disciples, if you have love for one another" (Jn 13:35).

Although the Christian faith always takes into account the reality of sin and always extends understanding and compassion to human failure, it is the high moral quality of the lives of its individual members that helps to make the Church a powerful, leavening sign of God's love in the world.

"In this way, the children of God and the children of the devil are made plain; no one who fails to act in righteousness belongs to God, nor anyone who does not love his brother" (1 Jn 3:10).

Preaching, therefore, reveals the moral expectations of the gospel in order to build up the community of believers as a true sign of God's presence and action. Catholic businessmen, for example, should stand out from the crowd because of their exemplary financial practices. Catholic families should reflect the values of the Christian community and thereby become sources of strength to families who have not yet entered into the believing community.

Finally, the Christian community as a community should undertake social programs to ensure that individual efforts at loving are brought to fruitful completion. A question: Is the Catholic community a leader in social reform in areas of need? Does the entire community reflect gospel love for the unloveable?

The need for preaching that stresses the moral values of the Christian community is underscored by the National Conference of Catholic Bishops in the document issued in 1974, *A Review of the Principal Trends in the Life of the Catholic Church in the United States:*

"For a large number of Catholics the influence of secular society—and all that implies, for good as well as ill—counts more heavily than the influence of the Church."

If this be true, and we have no reason to believe the bishops are wrong, we know that the Church is not the sign it should be for our generation. To correct this lamentable situation, the Second Vatican Council taught:

"Profound and rapid changes make it particularly urgent that no one, ignoring the trend of events or drugged by laziness, content himself with a merely individualistic morality. It grows increasingly true that the obligations of justice and love are fulfilled only if each person, contributing to the common good, according to his own abilities and the needs of others, also promotes and assists the public and private institutions dedicated to bettering conditions of human life" (*Pastoral Constitution on the Church in the Modern World*, No. 30).

Effective preaching to build community moral values will eventually result, by God's grace, in the community becoming a beacon of light to those living in the darkness of sin and despair, and the Church will be a potent source of influence to transform society.

The best example of the changes in society brought about by the preaching of the Church is found in the adoption by the larger society of the Christian concept of marriage.

The Roman concept of marriage was quite similar to the age-old notion of marriage in the ancient near east: the husband and wife were not equals in the relationship. Rather, the wife was a dependent of her husband, a daughter, as it were. In Roman society, it was both socially and legally acceptable for a husband to have a concubine, but the wife who had relations with another man could be condemned to death. Furthermore, abortion, exposure of infants, and divorce were common because marriage really existed for the good of the state.

Contrary to the prevailing view, the Christians insisted that husbands be faithful to their wives, that children were a gift of God to be nurtured by both parents in the love of God, and that the marriage relationship—the union of the two in one flesh—was good in itself because God was its author. It is difficult today to fully appreciate the revolutionary nature of this Christian teaching; yet, this apparently powerless group, through the preaching and teaching of its leaders, managed to make the old view of marriage unattractive to their listeners.

The early Christian preachers were not afraid to challenge the authorities whom they essentially respected in other matters, and that challenge, flowing from the preaching of revealed truth, eventually resulted in profound and lasting social changes. In addition to the teaching on marriage, the preachers forbade their Christian followers to have anything to do with the worship of the Roman gods. They demanded of them adherence to a code of sexual morality that differed radically from that of the secular society. Finally, Christianity challenged the ancient institution of slavery, holding that slaves, like freemen, had souls and deserved respect.

By its preaching that God was not just a disinterested mystical super-human, as commonly believed by the pagans of the time, but a transcendent personal Creator whose essence is love, Christianity was able to reform society because it reformed the believer's personal relationship with God.

Evangelization: Sharing Faith with Others
Jesus said to his disciples:
"You will receive power when the holy Spirit comes upon you, and you will be my witnesses in Jerusalem, throughout Judea and Samaria, and to the ends of the earth" (Acts 1:8).

This is the crowning activity that marks the believing community. It seeks to reach out, as did the Church of Jerusalem, to proclaim the gospel to the entire world. Evangelization, as Pope Paul VI said so eloquently, brings the power of the gospel to all levels of society and transforms humanity from within making it a new creation.[7]

Preaching, therefore, should inspire the faithful to share their faith with those who do not yet believe. As a result of hearing the word of God preached by their pastors, the Christian community should design active programs in evangelization as a priority for itself.

As we will see in Chapter Six, the ability to be effective in evangelization depends on the formation of the entire Christian community in gospel values. When the community has been properly formed by the preaching of the word of God, it will, by the power of the gospel itself, reach out to share with others the gifts the Lord has given his people.

Unfortunately, statistics tell us that at the present time evangelization is not a priority in the Church: not nationally, not in dioceses, not in parishes. In recent years, growth of the Church through conversion has been less than one-fifth of one percent per year.

Pope Paul VI recognized the problem as far back as 1970, when he said:

"If the faith fails to find hearers and believers, is it not because it is taught and preached in an old, abstruse way, cut off from life and contrary to the tendencies and tastes of today? Ought we not renew the kerygma—the announcement of the Christian message—if we want to find hearers and followers?" (*Address of September 16, 1970*).

Preaching aimed at forming a Christian community that will evangelize the world begins with a reexamination of the gospel in terms that are understood and valued by contemporary Christians. When the Christian community is itself being renewed by the word of God, it will seek new ways to communicate the ancient deposit of faith.

NOTES

1. "Peace on Earth" (*Pacem in Terris*) in *The Papal Encyclicals*, Vol. 5. 1958–1981, ed. by Claudia Carlen, I.H.M. (New York: McGrath Publishing Company, 1981), pp. 107–129.

2. *Constitution on the Sacred Liturgy*, No. 10.

3. Cf. Matthew 5:16.

4. In fact, this great doctor of the spiritual life notes that difficulty in loving comes from basically two sources: first, from the sheer scope or magnitude of the work to be accom-

plished in the act of loving; second, from the fact that I am
not really willing to perform the act of love with a "ready
will." My reluctance, therefore, makes it difficult to do good
and love well, and at the same time, since I am lacking motivation, the result of doing the difficult deed is not really
meritorious. Cf. *Summa Theologiae* I–II, q. 114, a. 4, ad 2; II–
II, q. 28, a. 7, and a. 8, ad 2.

5. Cf. 1 Corinthians 11:17–34.

6. Cf. 1 Thessalonians 1:7–10; 3:12–4:12.

7. *Apostolic Exhortation on Evangelization in the Modern World,*
No. 18.

Preaching the Gospel to the Modern World

In the two thousand year history of the Church, it is clear that it has succeeded in bearing witness to Christ because it has been a powerful influence for good both in terms of the personal lives of individuals and the life of society as a whole.

Nevertheless, in recent years, in spite of the Spirit-filled efforts of the Second Vatican Council and individual bishops, priests, and laity, the western world is slow in responding to the message of Christ.

There are many reasons for this negative attitude in our society today. We live in complex times with many philosophical systems competing for the allegiance of mankind. Christianity is deeply divided by denominationalism. Aware of the dangers of radical internal division, a succession of Popes has reaffirmed the essential unity of revealed truth. The latest one to do so is Pope John Paul II, who, in his first encyclical, *Redeemer of Man* (*Redemptor hominis*), said:

"In this field of human knowledge, which is continually being broadened and yet differentiated, faith too must be investigated deeply, manifesting the magnitude of revealed mystery and tending towards an understanding of truth, which has in God its one supreme source. If it is permissible and even desirable that the enormous work to be done in this direction should take into consideration a certain pluralism of methodology, the work cannot however depart from the fundamental unity in the teaching of Faith and Morals which is that work's end. Accordingly, close collaboration by theology with the Magisterium is indispensable" (*Redeemer of Man*, No. 19).

Granted the complexity of the situation and the diversity of causes that brought it into being, one major cause of the present lack of response is that the message of the gospel is not being heard by people, Catholics or not, because preachers are not adequately relating it to their hearers' own experience.

When former Beatle John Lennon was killed, *The New Yorker* magazine wrote:

"Many complicated explanations have been given and will continue to be given for the depth of grief that people all over the world have felt at the death of John Lennon, but one explanation may be quite simple. Beyond Lennon's great gifts as a composer, poet, and performer, beyond, and in spite of, his unparalleled and burdensome celebrity, he remained truly a man of the spirit—this humorous and friendly man who held on to his humanity against awesome odds, and who did not lecture us but, rather, spoke to us quietly, and in ways that we all understood. In what he said directly, in what he said in his very beautiful songs, and in the way he tried to live his far too brief life, the message that came through—and how rarely we hear such a message—was: Be peaceful, be loving, be gentle."

Even if one recognizes a certain media hyperbole in the reaction to Lennon's tragic death, the fact remains that his death touched many because his message was valued by many. In the midst of a complex world, he did manage to win a hearing, and if one credits *The New Yorker* at all, he won a hearing for the message the Church also proclaims: "Be peaceful, be loving, be gentle."

The gospel truths are clearly, lucidly expressed in articulate terms that have been nurtured and matured by the careful scrutiny of intellectual analysis for twenty centuries. Indeed, Catholicism seems most attractive to the intellectually capable. Today, studies indicate, most American converts to Roman Catholicism are relatively well-educated, almost one-fourth having attended college. Yet, for all its intellectual appeal, the annual convert rate in our country has been running at less than one-fifth of one percent for years.

Why, then, is the Church not being heeded by a world that is in such turmoil and suffering so intensely and yet responds so movingly to an event like the death of John Lennon?

One of the reasons may be that preachers have more concern for their own agenda than the people's agenda.[1] That is, they focus attention on what they think the people need to hear rather than on what the people know they need to hear. And no matter how hard the preacher insists, unless the listeners are disposed to hear what he is saying, they will not really hear his message. It is not a question of rejecting what the preacher says, the listeners will not have even listened to it enough to reject it.

This fundamental truth about communication is commonly experienced by everyone who has spent any time watching television. *TV Guide* reported:

"Most of us simply snap on the set rather than select a show. The first five minutes are spent prospecting channels, looking for gripping images."[2]

Viewers shop for shows, and they stop shopping only when they are interested by what they see. No matter what the quality of the program, the determining factor in turning it on is the viewer's interest in it.

Assuring audience interest and, therefore, attention or "tuning in" to the word of God requires the presence of a number of factors, and in the previous chapters we have discussed some of them. Among the most important elements in fruitful preaching are the insights into the meaning of divine revelation that are being communicated because they are the substance of preaching and the reason one wants to hear preaching to begin with.

THE KEY TO AUDIENCE ATTENTION

Contemporary research in communication theory tells us that the real key to attracting and holding a congregation's attention is relevance. In their article, "Exploring Some Correlates of Sermon Impact on Catholic Parishioners," Pargament and Silverman conclude:

"The degree to which the cleric attempts to relate his sermons to the life experiences of the members was the most potent predictor [of sermon impact]."[3]

The skill with which the preacher shows how his insights are connected to the lives of his audience in terms of their daily, ordinary and complex lives is the most important element in successful preaching. In order to be listened to, the preacher has to show the people that he is talking about something they have been experiencing in their lives and that what he is talking about can help them exchange that experience for something that is more positively beneficial to them.

The questions we all ask subconsciously when a speaker begins to address us is: Why should I listen to you? How are your words going to benefit me? How is my life going to be changed for the better? To put it bluntly, we ask the unexpressed but real question: So what? And we will not listen for long if the speaker does not answer our very blunt question very quickly.

Notice, our attitude toward the speaker and his message is not the result of a deliberate act of the mind flowing out of good will or bad will. That would take some time for analysis. Our reaction is as instantaneous as it is instinctive. Even the young child reacts the same way before he has the capacity to analyze why he should listen or not listen. It is a preconscious movement on the mind to protect itself from boredom or information overload, the working of a natural and necessary defense mechanism. It is the television viewer's shopping for the gripping image.

KNOWING THE LISTENERS

Given this communication dynamic, the first step in preparing to preach effectively is to answer the question: What are my listeners going through—experiencing—that will make them *want* to listen to me talk about this subject? When the preacher is able to answer that question clearly and firmly, he will know how to structure his sermon so that his audience will listen to his insights, understand them, and relate them to their lives. The content itself, and his urgency to communicate it, will determine the form and structure of his preaching.

For example, say you are a leader of a charismatic prayer group or, perhaps, its pastor. You know that the members of the group come to the prayer meetings to experience inner healing. You know they hunger deeply to learn how they can put greater trust in the Spirit and discern more clearly his working in their lives. But you also know that there are disturbances in the group.

You have an excellent model for grappling with the group's needs and problems in the great apostle, Paul. In his letters to the Corinthians, for example, we see that Paul knew the difficulties his new converts were encountering, and he addressed them directly. He provided just the right aspects of the word of God to heal the wounds of the community. It was not an easy task; Paul was not immediately successful. Some vigorously opposed him and spoke against him. But his teachings were ultimately effective.

Like Paul, all effective preachers adapt their message to their hearers and their experience of life. They begin their preaching, in other words, with the people and not with the preacher's message.

An all too common example of failing to reach the listeners is the Sunday homily when the homilist starts with the text of the day instead of reflecting his interest in what concerns his people. Only after he has exposed the text, and perhaps recapitulated it, does the homilist "apply" it to the needs of the people. By that time, most of the people have long stopped listening.

Or again, so often people who are suffering intensely want to know: What does God want from me? The preacher can tell them. He cannot always be specific about what God wants here and now, and for him to try to do so is a serious error. It leads to simplistic applications of specific texts that results in "good advice" preaching. Good advice preaching is usually discounted by the mature listener.

In Good News preaching, on the other hand, the preacher reveals the divine will in general terms, which the Holy Spirit then applies to the individual in the particular circumstances of his own life. Grace moves the individual to discern the meaning of the events in his life because he intuits God's purpose for him personally in the light of his vocation.

The Bishop's Committee on Priestly Life and Ministry of the United States Catholic Conference addressed the question of the Sunday homily in its excellent document, *Fulfilled In Your Hearing: The Homily in the Sunday Assembly*, as follows:

"Unless a preacher knows what a congregation needs, wants, or is able to hear, there is every possibility that the message offered in the homily will not meet the needs of the people who hear it. To say this is by no means to imply that preachers are only to preach what their congregations want to hear. . . . Homilists may indeed preach on what they understand to be the real issues, but if they are not in touch with what the people think are the real issues, they will very likely be misunderstood or not heard at all. What is communicated is not what is said, but it is what is heard, and what is heard is determined in large measure by what the hearer needs or wants to hear" (p. 4).

THE PROCESS OF COMMUNICATION

The principles we have been explaining reduce themselves to the process of homily and sermon construction. This process must be carried out in all forms of preaching: evangelization, catechesis, didascalia, or liturgical, in one preaching event or many. It is required in one-to-one conversations with perspective converts; it forms the basis for a course of religious education. It structures whole retreats and missions as well as the sermons within them.

This process is used to identify the elements that need to be presented in any form of preaching if it is to enlighten minds or touch hearts and change lives. The actual communication will take a variety of forms that will be determined by many factors: the occasion, the time available, the persons addressed, and so on.

It must be stressed that in this book we are discussing preaching, not academic lectures, journal articles, essays, or theological treatises. Unfortunately, preachers have adopted the structures of other forms of communication, especially the academic lecture, too readily, and they do not succeed in holding the audience's attention.

Identify the Human Felt Need
The first step is carefully to identify the issue that the preacher is going to address. It should be a real problem that people are experiencing in their lives, something that they are going through, mentally, physically or emotionally. Perhaps it is the hurt for which they seek healing by the word of God. It should be of sufficient depth that it captivates interest and attention.

The first step, then, is to be aware of the concerns of the listeners, not simply to impose the preacher's personal views on them. If the preacher knows there is something the people should hear, he has to locate their felt need that will allow them to turn their attention to what he knows "they need to know." This point will be more fully discussed in Chapter Ten.

Illustrate the Felt Need
Secondly, the issue, question, or experience should be clearly illustrated so that the audience recognizes that what the preacher is about to discuss is a realistic situation that most of them have been experiencing in their own lives. The purpose of illustrations, which can be case histories, statistics and what they signify, or the preacher's own experience, is to make the problem vivid and easily recognizable by the audience.

If the problem is real and significant, one vivid illustration will be enough to arouse the interest of the listeners. Thus, the first two steps, while of maximum importance, need not consume much time in the actual presentation. If the preacher speaks to a true felt need of his listeners, they will be able to fill in the details from their own experience.

Develop the Solution

The third element is the solution to the problem the audience has been experiencing and the preacher has just exemplified. He shows that what he is proposing is truly the feasible, realistic solution to the problem outlined, so that his gospel message will successfully answer the question, heal the hurt, meet the need.

This third element constitutes the major portion of the oral communication. It contains the insights that the preacher himself has developed; it should utilize the greatest proportion of time available. Here the preacher will draw upon Scripture, theology, the documents of the Church, contemporary research, and the human experience of other persons to support his basic statements.

Illustrate the Solution

Finally, the preacher illustrates his solution so that it is clear to his hearers that the solution he is proposing is a workable one and that it indeed answers the need that had been so vividly illustrated at the beginning of his communication.

EXAMPLES OF THE ELEMENTS OF ORAL COMMUNICATION

Premarital Sex

In his excellent book, *Psychology as Religion,* Paul C. Vitz[4] argues persuasively that the psychological environment of society today has pretty much convinced many people that they are basically good and have an absolute right to determine for themselves what they should or should not do. Individual freedom in all things—including morality—rests on the isolated conscious self as the sole judge of what the self should value and how it should act.

Furthermore, because we live in a scientifically and technologically oriented culture, the analytical attitude that dominates science and technology has tended to isolate the individual from many of the social bonds that result from cultural and religious traditions, community structure, and the family.

This cultural formation is not a conscious response to information or teaching. Rather, it is a premoral condition of life in which people make their subsequent moral judgments. This means that at a rather profound psychological level, many of us operate on the principle that no one has a right to tell us what to do. We seek guidance, advice, and counsel, but in the last instance we have to make our own decisions free from the imposition of values by others. In fact, if one is told "you must," that person feels subconsciously that an effort is being made to manipulate him or her. No one, such people feel, has the right to do that: not parents, not society, and not the Church.

This premoral state of mind, something which all of us, at least to some degree, accept as a first principle for judging certain acquired information, has significant effects upon the acceptance of the gospel message. It is a contributing factor to the rather widespread resistance among many Catholics to the Church's teaching.

There is a certain dynamics of communication at work when Catholic catechists and preachers seek to communicate Christian sexual values to those shaped by today's cultural values. Because these latter are based on dubious first principles, real communication that will change ideas, values and life-style is all but impossible between the two sets of values. Therefore, the preacher's first step is to establish what first principles activate his listeners. And then: How can I get them to give me a serious hearing?

When a Catholic preacher these days begins to tell teenagers that premarital sex is morally offensive to God, large numbers simply are not able to "hear" him. The preacher's words come from an alien perspective of life, so they are dismissed. The young people may respect the preacher (read here: priest, catechist, parent) for being honest and expressing his opinion, but they will only consider it his opinion or "the Church's" opinion. It will be, however, irrelevant to the way they think and act in today's "enlightened" world. Given the secular psychological and ethical formation to which they are subjected, teenagers perceive premarital sex as merely one more experience in a series of experiences that are necessary for creative personal growth. Sex is an expression of caring, so if one cares outside of marriage, who is to say it is morally reprehensible? Successful sex, in fact, assures the sexually active that they are becoming complete persons.

What does the preacher (homilist, catechist, evangelist, parent) do to communicate the gospel message about premarital sex to young people today in the face of such a powerful formative influence as that of contemporary society?

Using the principle of need identification, a possible approach would be for the preacher to show that the reason young people are having difficulties in their relationships with other human beings is precisely because premarital sex harms both themselves and their partners. The preaching can show the wretched consequences of this practice in young lives, drawing upon the experiences of the young themselves. Contemporary journalism and sociological study offer numerous examples that can serve as an effective basis for Christian preaching in this area.

One of the reasons so many children follow the sexual mores of the times is because their parents did not communicate the faith to them. Instead of devoting time to establishing common Christian principles that could be interiorized by their children and serve as the firm basis for Christian behavior, many parents merely imposed religious practices, such as Mass attendance, upon their children without spending enough time in inculcating the basic meaning of religious values. Neither did they accurately ascertain what their children really thought about life in general.

Mass Attendance

The practical issue in passing on a life of faith to one's children is not whether a child *has* to go Mass, or *has* to say his prayers, sin or not, or whether he is setting a good example for his younger brothers and sisters. The point at issue is how to help the child *want* to go to Mass, *want* to say prayers. One of the best ways to turn *have to* into *want to* is for the parents to set the example by their own behavior toward God and the Church.

Love of Neighbor

Jesus said to the rich young man, "You must love your neighbor as yourself." Today, if some people loved their neighbor as they loved themselves, their neighbor would be in deep trouble. Varying forms of self-hatred are common, and a lack of healthy self-love is doing great harm to relationships between people.[5] It is pointless, therefore, for the preacher to stress the necessity of loving one's neighbor, if, in fact, the real problem his listener is experiencing is loving himself. The one who hates himself is trapped in self-hatred, and no one can love anybody else until he experiences himself as being loved first.

Jesus exemplified his teaching about love of neighbor with the parable of the Good Samaritan. However, if the listeners live in an environment in which muggings, gang wars, break-ins, murders create a fear of human relationships, they will not really be able to "hear" the story as a parable of love. They will hear it as an impossible demand, or perhaps at best they will hear it as an unrealistic vision, but their experience of life will prevent them from hearing it in terms of a love that they themselves are capable of giving to another person.

The homilist, therefore, who begins simply with an explanation of the gospel text and then merely exhorts his listeners to imitate the Good Samaritan will scarcely affect them. He must first preach the word of God in a way that frees his hearers from their self-hatred and fears so that they will be able to hear Jesus' parable as a revelation of love and a practical guide by which to achieve their own earthly and eternal destinies.

Loneliness

Loneliness today has reached epidemic proportions. For millions, loneliness is a daily, excruciating agony. Many end their loneliness by taking their own lives. Others think that their loneliness will end when others begin to love them, pay them the heed they desire, respect them as persons. They spend their lives, therefore, buying love from others. Children are encouraged to "show off" in front of their parent's friends; women bestow sexual favors; men pick up the tab.

The fact of the matter, however, is that a person is lonely, not because others have failed to love them, but because they have failed to love others. It is only in loving others that we establish communion with them. Others might love me, but if I do not love them, there is still no communion, and I remain locked in my own world, sad and lonely.

A preacher, therefore, cannot begin to preach effectively to lonely people about loving others if he does not first speak of their experience of loneliness. The abstract notion of loving others can seem very abstract and distant to the lonely person whose life is governed by the pain of being alone. It is the preacher's task to connect the pain of loneliness with its remedy —a reaching out to others, in spite of pain, in love.

For example, recent Christian immigrants to this country are experiencing an intense uprooting from all they hold dear and familiar. The consequences of war and economic deprivation have torn thousands of Asian and Latin American immigrants (legal or illegal) from their native culture and plunked them down in a totally new and alien environment. They are finding it to be a most difficult period of adjustment. As a result, many members of even large families are profoundly lonely, and whole groups of families and individuals are experiencing bouts of deep depression.

Preachers who simply preach to them about the necessity of adjusting to the new environment are not helping them integrate themselves into their new way of life, which will, no doubt, be a permanent way of life for themselves and their children. Neither are they helping them to overcome their loneliness. These immigrant lonely are not able to hear such exhortations because of their pain.

The preacher, however, who is able to show that he is no stranger to their experiences will then be able to focus their attention on the gospel message of loving others as Christ loved on the cross. Having established his sensitivity to their pain, he will be able to show them how their reaching out, even in an alien culture, will deliver them from loneliness and depression. First, though, the communality of experience must be established by acknowledging the hurt before the healing word of God can be applied to the festering wound of human isolation. If the preacher fails to do this, his listeners will simply not "hear" the gospel truth.

PROBLEM AREAS IN PREACHING

The Bishops' Agenda

In a commencement address delivered at The Catholic University of America on May 19, 1984, Reverend J. Brian Hehir, Secretary for Social Development and World Peace at the United States Catholic Conference, speaking of the "public Church," that is, the Catholic witness to contemporary policy issues, said:

"Four questions—nuclear strategy, abortion, Central America, and the economy—form the heart of the public policy agenda in the United States today."

His point was that because these four issues call for witness by the Church, the bishops are addressing these issues forcefully in their public policy statements.

On the other hand, there is evidence that these issues are not of such concern to ordinary Catholics that they are willing to become actively involved dealing with them as witnesses for Christ. In 1983, for example, fear of nuclear war was numbered as only seven in the list of major problems for teenagers.[6] Drug abuse, unemployment, and alcohol abuse were issues of far greater concern. Other studies of parish life[7] indicate that parishioners want their church to be more concerned about family life and the passing on of faith to their children. If these are the real issues for the faithful, the question preachers need to answer, therefore, is: How can we make this agenda of the bishops the agenda for individual Christians who comprise the Church, "public" or otherwise?

For this agenda of the bishops to be translated into effective Church teaching, preachers will have to make it relevant to the daily experiences of the people, believers and nonbelievers, who are seeking truth to live by. Preachers will have to show, for example, a clear connection between the word of God, an increase of faith, and the political-social events in Central America. Or, they will have to relate living in the Kingdom of God to the American economic policies.

Preaching on Birth Control

Since the development of new technologies for birth prevention and the great rise in world populations, there has been considerable debate in Church circles regarding the morality of using artificial birth control devices. In March, 1963, Pope John XXIII instituted a special commission composed of experts and married couples to investigate the question. In spite of the fact that the majority of Pope John XXIII's commission recognized the morality of using such devices, five years later, on July 25, 1968, Pope Paul VI issued the encyclical letter *Humanae Vitae* that banned as immoral the use of artificial birth control devices. In spite of some continuing opposition within the Catholic community, *Humanae Vitae* has become the normative teaching of the Church, which has been reaffirmed by Pope John Paul II. As a result, there is no question today that it is the official teaching of the Church. Nevertheless, this teaching continues to be questioned by numbers of theologians, marriage counselors, and married couples. Surveys have reported that 70 percent of practicing Catholics think Catholics should be allowed to use artificial birth control methods even though banned by Church teaching.

Clearly, then, there is often a discrepancy between what the Church teaches and what Catholics do. While there are many causes for this phenomenon, one cannot help but feel that preaching has not communicated to the Catholic people in a realistic way, and in the light of their experienced need to limit births, the advantages of avoiding artificial contraception devices and using only natural family planning methods. Preachers seem to have failed to make at least this aspect of Christian teaching relevant to the people.

Bishops' Letters
Another example of the need for making the Christian message relevant occurs when a letter from the bishop is read in the parish churches at the Sunday Masses.[8]

The assumption is that if the letter is read aloud, the people will listen to it and derive from it the meaning the bishop intends to communicate. As one might imagine, this is an unjustified assumption. No one can force anyone to listen; the hearer has to be motivated to do so. Therefore, what the bishop's letter teaches must be introduced by pointing out certain needs of the people that will be addressed and, one may hope, be met, when the letter is read.

IDENTIFYING FELT NEEDS
In order, then, to motivate the listeners to attend to the word of God, the preacher has to know their felt needs. The preacher has to be in possession of rather detailed knowledge of the people to whom he is speaking. This is equally true of the homilist at Sunday liturgy, the catechist in his classroom or the leader of the Bible sharing group, the evangelist in his witness activities and, certainly, parents in passing on the faith to their children. The preacher has to know "where his audience is at." How does he find out?

Sacred Scripture

The first place to turn to analyze the human condition and, therefore, the experience of the contemporary audience is Sacred Scripture. God knows the hearts of his people better than anyone, and in his Scriptures, he has shown our human nature and human motivation at odds with his word and in accord with it.

The basic reality of the human condition and the source of all our pain and suffering is that we are sinners. We do not go about deliberately "committing sins" all day long, but we are sinners because we live more by illusions than by God's truth. Too often we act by passion: fear, greed, anger. We are driven to be totally independent and self-sufficient. We really want to do it all ourselves.

This passage from the Letter to the Ephesians sums up the human experience of sin:

"You were dead in your transgressions and sins in which you once lived following the age of this world, following the ruler of the power of the air, the spirit that is now at work in the disobedient. All of us once lived among them in the desires of our flesh, following the wishes of the flesh and the impulses, and we were by nature children of wrath, like the rest" (Eph 2:1–3).

Sin in the sense just defined is one thing the preacher has in common with his listeners, and the listeners have in common with one another. The word of God the preacher needs to hear is the word of God the people need to hear. In other words, if the preacher knows how to listen to himself when he preaches, the people may also listen to him. Listening to his own heart respond to the word of God he proclaims is perhaps the preacher's best test for the effectiveness of his message.

For example, there was a preacher who was preaching to a graduating class. It was to be a very elegant affair, and he had worked hard on his sermon. However, even as he was preparing it, he was sensitive to the fact that a lot of the things he was saying did not really interest him personally. He found himself speaking to the class about "being the hope of the future" and "meeting the challenge" because he thought these ideas were expected of him, but they seemed stale and did not really excite him. When, however, he was working on the parts of his text that developed his own experienced insights into the meaning of Scripture, he found his own heart quickening.

While he was actually preaching at the graduation, he became acutely conscious that his audience was drifting away from him during those moments when he had drifted away himself, but they were listening when he was speaking about matters that had truly been important for his own life of faith. At last he decided to omit the dull spots. He went directly to the points that had appealed to him. Afterwards one of the school officials came up and said to him: "I have to be honest, Father. I was really tuning out in the beginning, but then you really got on my wavelength, and I hung on every word. You were great!"

Sociological Data
In addition to the biblical analysis of the human condition, there are many other resources available to the preacher to help him identify the painful experiences contemporary men and women are having, and which require the preaching of God's word for healing. There are many fine sociological studies on cultural influences and contemporary attitudes. There are excellent books on psychology and the psychological environment.

For example, sociological studies of the Catholic
Church in the United States indicate that most conversions to Catholicism take place between the ages of 20
to 30 (46 percent), most who drop out do so by age 25
(54 percent), and most returnees are between 20 and
35. These statistics indicate that the age when most
people are most concerned about exploring religious
questions is between 15 to 35.[9]

As a result, preaching can have the greatest influence
on persons between their middle teens and before
they reach 30. The Lord is calling the young to be
members of his chosen people. The young are the
ones who have the interest in joining and the desire to
belong to a community. (Consider the "gang" and cult
phenomena.) The young are God's children who are
looking for the meaning of their lives that only the
gospel can give them.

Pope John Paul said of youth:
"[It] is the time of a particularly intense discovery of
the human 'I' and the properties and capacities connected with it. . . . The treasure which is youth is the
treasure of discovering, organizing, choosing, foresee-
ing and making the first personal decisions, decisions
that will be important for the future in the strictly personal dimension of human existence" (*Apostolic Letter
to the Youth of the World*, March 31, 1985).

Urging priests to have a great love for young people
as an integral part of their priestly ministry, the Pope
wrote *To all the Priests of the Church for Holy Thursday,
1985:*

"The current year 1985 through the initiative of the
United Nations Organization is in fact being celebrated
throughout the world as *International Youth Year.* It has
seemed to me that this initiative should not remain on
the margins of the Church, any more than other noble

initiatives of an international character of the Year of the Aged, or the Year of the Disabled and others. In all these initiatives, the Church cannot remain on the sidelines, for the essential reason that they are at the heart of her mission and service, which is to be built up and to grow as the community of believers."

In both letters, the Pope commented extensively on the story of Christ's meeting with the young man who had great possessions to explain the qualities required to preach effectively to the young.[10] In short, preachers should consciously direct their attention to the young. They should illustrate their preachings, whatever form they take, with examples suitable to the experience of the young. They should express the scriptural teachings in language understood easily by persons in that younger age group. As Pope John Paul said:

"The time of youth in the life of every person is a particularly responsible phase. Love for young people is above all awareness of this responsibility and readiness to share it" (Holy Thursday Letter).

The parish community can manifest its love for the young and share in their responsibility by celebrating liturgies that are attractive to young people and that will dispose them to listen to the word of God. At the same time, a well-directed liturgical homily can be of immense benefit in helping the young participate fully and faithfully in the liturgy. Both preaching and liturgy will strengthen them for active involvement in the life of the community. To belong to a group is a hunger of the young; their hunger can be satisfied by belonging to a vibrant Christian community formed and nourished by the word of God.

Other studies that report on what qualities parishioners think a Christian community should have, what services it should offer, what activities it should undertake, and what interpersonal relationships it should foster. Understanding his peoples' needs and expectations is essential for a pastor to successfully create a cohesive and cooperative community through the preaching of the word of God.

Church members are looking for warm and personal parishes in which they experience a sense of responsibility and have an opportunity to participate in parish activities.[11]

While they want open relationships with everyone in the parish, parishioners especially want to feel free to approach their priests and the parish staff. Consequently, it is important to the people that their priests be personable and easy to talk with.

The leadership of a good parish community should be marked by stability and consistency because sociological data indicates that frequent changes in parish personnel are detrimental to the building of community.

Parishioners have also expressed their preference for a variety of liturgical celebrations and parish activities. The latter activities should be designed to provide support for family living that is under such attack by certain tendencies in society today. In fact, people belong to a church or do not belong mainly because of their family life or parent-child relationships.

When these significant findings about parishioners' expectations, family relationships, and the young age at which much religious activity takes place are combined, parish preachers have a basic profile of the people whom they are trying to reach. It says that, in general, preaching programs have to be oriented toward meeting the felt needs of the family and the young.

The contemporary preacher has to read widely in other fields besides sociology and psychology, of course, to better understand why his listeners are the way they are and respond to his preaching the way they do. In addition to the psychological pressures on hearers of the gospel today that Vitz has analyzed so well, there are also the severe cultural pressures that Robert Bellah and his colleagues analyzed so effectively.[12] The preacher will be able to recognize these influences and appreciate their impact on the lives of his listeners by reading extensively in history, anthropology, politics, and art.

Group Reflections

After reading in these areas, it is helpful for the parish preachers to join together in small group discussions to reflect on how cultural values help or impede the hearing of the gospel proclamation today. The following questions have served to stimulate such reflection by some preachers and preaching teams:

1. What is the modern American's greatest source of personal fulfillment?
2. What are his/her criteria for success?
3. About what does he/she get truly enthusiastic?
4. What are his/her most enjoyable moments?
5. What activity(ies) occupies most of his/her time, talent, energies?
6. What are his/her dicta of morality?
7. What are the symbols that have significance for the modern American?
8. What strikes him/her as amusing?
9. To what does he/she consistently devote his/her leisure time?
10. What is the major source of his/her value judgments?
11. What are his/her popular devotions and beliefs?
12. What does the modern American fear most?
13. What does he/she want from life?
14. What does he/she expect from life?
15. How does he/she experience the presence of evil?

As useful and necessary as general sociological data
are for understanding the contemporary environment
in which preaching takes place, parish preachers need
to know as specifically as possible the felt needs and
expectations of their own immediate community. A
useful tool for acquiring this kind of information is a
Parish Survey Questionnaire in which the parishioners
are asked to provide basic information about their attitudes, motivations, and desires. The following series
of questions form one possible model. The answers
the people supply to them will be effective in planning
the parish preaching:

1. Why do you come to church on Sunday?
2. What do you want your priest to do for you?
3. What do you want your parish community to do
for you?
4. What do you like best about Sunday Mass?
5. What do you like best about your priest?
6. What do you like least about Sunday Mass?
7. What do you like least about your priest?

Other questions could be added to gain information
about catechetical programs, liturgical practices, evangelization ministries, family care, and the like. The list
given here is certainly a very limited one, but the answers to it will illustrate how necessary it is to know
the listeners' reactions to preaching in order actually
to touch their lives. The information gleaned should
be shared with parish committees who, in turn,
should form parish teams to assist the pastor in the
preaching of the gospel through homily planning meetings and catechetical and evangelization programs.

RELATING GOSPEL TRUTH TO FELT NEEDS
After the felt needs have been adequately and accurately identified, the preacher still has the task of

showing how different aspects of the gospel message can release the hurting persons from their painful prison.

The following schema proposes certain scriptural-theological themes that are especially pertinent to the experienced needs of the listeners. The schema is by no means exhaustive; nor is the listing in order of importance. Finally, no indication of the amount of time needed for the development of each element is indicated, since any development must be adapted to the particular circumstances of the listeners and to the total structure of the parish preaching program, about which we will have more to say in Chapter Ten.

The structure of the schematic presentation is simple. The left-hand column lists the experience of reality that figures prominently in the life of the listener. The right-hand column identifies some particular aspect of the gospel message in theological terminology that is particularly relevant to the experience of the listener.

For example, in the first instance, the listener has not had a strong experience of being loved. As a result, he lives under a nagging fear that he will be rejected. To compensate for this anxiety, he is driven to a variety of behavior patterns that may be in opposition to the gospel's teachings.

One way the preacher can approach the problem of fear is to preach the eternal and gracious love of God for each human being he has created. This entire doctrine of God's love for us is summed up in the theological technical term of "Predestination." It means simply that God loves us because he is love, and he has the power to make his love effective in our lives by making us capable of good and experiencing joy, peace and eternal life.

Felt Need of the Listener	*Gospel Element*

To the unaffirmed, fearful of rejection	Predestination
	Incarnation
	  Jesus as savior
	  His personal qualities
	  His power

To overachievers, semi-Pelegians	Grace Divine power The new creation of Paul
To those experiencing victimhood: through disease, loss, suffering, violence	The cross Value of suffering
To those experiencing guilt	Redemption Forgiveness Reconciliation Mercy
To those experiencing weakness, failure	Sin as an enslaving power Ongoing salvific action of God Spiritual interiorization by grace
To materialists, consumerists	The resurrection The life of faith Hope in glory
To rationalists, humanists	Life in the Holy Spirit Divine wisdom
To the ignorant and searching	The word of God Divine revelation

To the lonely	Realized eschatology
	Pauline mysticism
	Johannine vision
	The Church community
To the complacent and comfortable	Christian mission and service
	Evangelization

Felt Need: Area of Betterment

The problems, needs or hurts that are identified in the schema are not crises in every case. They can be simply long-endured, long-suffered conditions of individual life for which the gospel offers the healing remedy of truth and power. For example, blindness for a blind person is not a crisis, perhaps not even a problem, but it is a condition that is oppressive. The gift of sight would be most welcome to the one who is blind, even though barring a miracle, seeing again is not a realistic expectation. But through the power of the gospel, the blind person can live in joy and peace, even though he remains without physical sight.

The saving word of Jesus Christ is like sight to the blind. Just as sight betters human life, so God's word betters human life.

Jesus said:
"I am the light of the world. Whoever follows me will not walk in darkness, but will have the light of life" (Jn 8:12).

The identification of the felt need indicates that area of human life that will be bettered by following the teaching of Jesus. Fear is overcome by confidence, hate is overcome by love, anger is overcome by patience, and so on. Identifying the area of betterment helps the preacher avoid preaching moral negatives by encouraging him to emphasize the positive side of the gospel message.

For example, preachers will be more successful in motivating families to use natural planning methods by showing their desirability in terms of the experience of family and conjugal happiness than simply by condemning artificial birth control. To accuse a person of "being wrong" may or may not help him to lead a better life. At present, the evidence is that mere condemnation is not motivating some Catholics to give up artificial birth control.

Preaching must show how happiness in doing God's will is an attainable reality here and hereafter thanks to the free gift of salvation in Jesus Christ, our Lord.

NOTES

1. On May 2, 1986, three Vatican Secretariats (for Christian Unity, for Non-Christians and for Non-Believers) and the Pontifical Council for Culture issued a significant document, *Sects or New Religious Movements: A Pastoral Challenge*. It describes the challenge presented to the Church today by many conversions away from Catholicism to Fundamentalist Protestantism and other evangelical movements. It honestly admits that a major factor in the success of Fundamentalism in attracting Catholics is the Church's failure to meet the needs of those converted.

2. Quoted by David Marc in "Understanding Television" in *The Atlantic Monthly*, August, 1984, p. 42.

3. *Review of Religious Research*, Vol. 24, No. 1 (September, 1982).

4. Paul C. Vitz, *Psychology as Religion: The Cult of Self-Worship* (Grand Rapids, MI: Wm B. Eedermans, 1977).

5. See Conrad W. Barrs and Anna A. Terruwe, *Healing the Unaffirmed: Recognizing Deprivation Neurosis* (New York: Alba House, 1976). They stress that the lack of personal affirma-

tion is at the root of much of the psychological illness people are experiencing today—their "unaffirmed syndrome."

6. *Emerging Trends* (Princeton: Princeton Religion Research Center), Vol. 5, No. 8 (October, 1983).

7. Dean R. Hoge, *Converts, Dropouts, Returnees* (New York: Pilgrim Press, 1981).

8. The subject of the letter might be diocesan eucharistic regulations, Catholic education, diocesan funding, or some other uniquely important topic that merits the attention of all the faithful. Because there is abundant evidence that most Catholics read neither the diocesan newspaper, which reprints the letter, nor the parish bulletin, which also reprints the letter, a customary way the bishops have of communicating to their people on major issues is by mandating that their letters be read aloud, usually in their entirety, at all the Sunday Masses, even if this means the bishop's letter takes the place of the liturgical homily.

9. Hoge, op. cit.

10. Matthew 19:16–22; Mark 10:17–22; and Luke 18:18–23.

11. Hoge, op. cit., p. 168.

12. Robert N. Bellah, et al., *Habits of the Heart: Individualism and Commitment in American Life* (Berkeley: University of California Press, 1985). This is a well-researched and perceptively written sociological study of the contemporary American character.

Chapter Five

The Kinds of Preaching

As we have established, there are two correlative terms in preaching: (1) the word of God, which is proclaimed, and (2) faith, which the word of God causes, forms, or awakens in the listener.[1] On the basis of the level of faith that results, we can distinguish three kinds of preaching: evangelization, catechesis, and didascalia (higher wisdom) preaching.

These kinds of preaching are not discrete entities, clearly distinguished from one another. They mark progressive stages of proclamation, as it were, that bring about the continuing process of maturation in faith by the power of the word of God itself and the internal action of the Holy Spirit in the soul of the believer. When we speak of three kinds of preaching, therefore, we are not implying that the preacher can clearly separate his listeners into distinct categories and then direct his preaching solely to one of them. The stages of growth in faith blend and overlap in each of us. Nevertheless, the preacher must have some general appreciation of the level of faith development of the particular audience he is addressing.

EVANGELIZATION

Evangelization is the first and most basic kind of preaching. It is addressed to those who, for whatever reason, do not yet believe in Jesus. The Church sends missionaries to bring the gospel to people who have not yet had the opportunity to hear it. By evangelizing, the missionaries convert these people to Christ, implant the Church, and make possible their entrance into the kingdom of God.

The Gospel of John attributes to Jesus himself the requirements for entering the kingdom, which are the bases for both the Church's preaching and sacramental ministry:

"Amen, amen, I say to you, no one can see the kingdom of God without being born from above. . . . Amen, amen, I say to you, no one can enter the kingdom of God without being born of water and Spirit. What is born of flesh is flesh and what is born of spirit is spirit. . . . For God did not send his Son into the world to condemn the world, but that the world might be saved through him. Whoever believes in him will not be condemned, but whoever does not believe has already been condemned, because he has not believed in the name of the only Son of God" (Jn 3:3 ff.).

But evangelization needs also to be addressed to Catholics who are Catholics in name only. These are Catholics who have never experienced the power, joy, and serenity faith brings, in spite of the fact that they have been educated in the truths of their religion and value its traditions as having intellectual and historical worth.

Evangelization needs to be an integral part of religious education programs for high school students. Although they may be familiar with the facts of their religion in some rudimentary way, sociological data reveals that they do not experience the fruits of its teachings in their lives. They lack "any internalized faith."[2]

Such students, who may come from "good Catholic families," are frequently disciplinary problems for their religion teacher because they have no motivation to learn about something in which they simply do not

believe and have no real desire to practice. They constitute a captive, but by no means captured, audience,
and as soon as the religious education program has
been completed (perhaps at the time of confirmation),
they leave the Church. There is evidence that large
numbers of young dropouts never return to the practice of their faith; one authority puts the figure at almost one-third.[3] Certainly, a return is not something
the Church can count on.[4]

Evangelization, then, is the preaching of the word of
God that aims at giving birth to an internalized faith-
trust relationship to the Lord in those who have not
yet been converted or who have been only partially
converted.

CATECHESIS
When one has been converted to Christ by the grace
of God and through the hearing of his word, there is
an overwhelming sense of having received a unique
gift, a special treasure. Evangelization brings about the
first encounter with the mystery of Christ among us,
and, as a result of the gift of faith, life has new meaning and purpose. The new believer has new goals,
new understanding, and seeks greater union with the
object of his love.

St. Augustine converted to Christianity when he was
32; twelve years later, in 399, A.D., he wrote his classic
spiritual work, *Confessions*. In that touching account of
his intense spiritual and intellectual struggles and ultimate conversion, he writes a number of prayers to his
new Lord that praise God for the freeing movements
of grace in his heart.

"O Lord, I am Thy servant: I am Thy servant and the
son of Thy handmaid. Thou hast broken my bonds. I
will sacrifice to Thee the sacrifice of praise. Let my
heart and my tongue praise Thee, and let all my bones

say, O Lord, who is like to Thee? Let them say and do Thou answer me and say to my soul: I am thy salvation" (*Confessions*, Book IX, No. I).

Augustine goes on to write of his deliverance from the burden of sin and anxiety and his newly found friendship with God:

"Now my mind was free from the cares that had gnawed it, from aspiring and getting and weltering in filth and rubbing the scab of lust. And I talked with You as friends talk, my glory and my riches and my salvation, my Lord God" (ibid.).

The writings of Augustine have always been popular with devout Christian readers because they articulate for all of us the experience of God that we have when we live in faith. In particular, there is the painful awareness that although our spirit has been set free, our body is still trapped in its old ways and needs continued deliverance. Augustine writes:

"When once I shall be united to Thee [God] with all my being, there shall be no more grief and toil, and my life will be alive, filled wholly with Thee. Thou dost raise up him whom Thou dost fill; whereas being not yet filled with Thee I am a burden to myself" (op. cit., No. XXVIII).

Two hungers, therefore, consume the evangelized: a need to praise God and thank him for the gift that has been so graciously given; and an intense need to purify oneself and grow in holiness of mind and will. The newly born believer seeks to intensify his relationship to God in Christ Jesus and to participate more fully in the power faith has bestowed. The power that comes from faith provides both present help and eternal salvation. St. Paul writes:

"For one believes with the heart and so is justified, and one confesses with the mouth and so is saved. . . . The same Lord is Lord of all, enriching all who call upon him. For 'everyone who calls upon the name of the Lord will be saved' " (Rom 10:10–13).

The believer's hunger, which was first satisfied by the hearing of God's word, has grown by the hearing. The believer wants more. He also wants a deeper personal participation in the mystery of Christ among us.

Catechetical preaching then focuses on the living out of the newly professed faith in terms of the customs, tradition, doctrines, and practices of the believing community to which the acceptance of the gospel message has brought the believer.

Paul, for example, does not simply exhort the Colossians to try to live "in Christ" in some kind of abstract way that has no practical relationship with daily behavior. He reveals that through faith they are now rooted in Christ and, therefore, must act in all things according to his teachings.

"As you received Christ Jesus the Lord, walk in him, rooted in him and built upon him and established in the faith as you were taught, abounding in thanksgiving" (Col 2:6,7).

Two main elements are constitutive of catechetical preaching: (1) participation in the sacramental life of the believing community, and (2) growth in ordinary Christian morality. These aspects, consistently preached in catechesis, lead to both personal and corporate holiness as concrete expressions of community living.

Paul's earliest letter, to the Thessalonians, sums up, as it were, his catechesis of the Church he founded in Thessalonica:

"For God did not destine us for wrath, but to gain salvation through our Lord Jesus Christ, who died for us, so that whether we are awake or asleep we may live together with him. Therefore, encourage one another and build one another up, as indeed you do. . . . Be at peace among yourselves. . . . Admonish the idle, cheer the fainthearted, support the weak, be patient with all. See that no one returns evil for evil; rather, always seek what is good both for each other and for all. Rejoice always. Pray without ceasing. In all circumstances give thanks, for this is the will of God for you in Christ Jesus" (1 Thes 5:9–18).

DIDASCALIA

The first two types of preaching, called evangelization and catechesis, are derived from Greek words and are more or less commonly used and understood. Didascalia, however, is less familiar. It, too, is derived from a Greek term *didaskalia*, which means teaching. The teaching that it refers to in New Testament usage is the authoritative teachings of Jesus as the revelation of the will of God. In the Pastoral Letters, *disdaskalia* becomes the sum of Christ's teachings.[5]

Jesus himself is the *Didaskalos* or Teacher (*Rabbi* in Hebrew). It is the title most frequently applied to him. The Teacher gathers around him disciples who become imbued with his teachings and, in their turn, become teachers to others.

As we are using the term here, didascalia signifies that kind of preaching of the word of God that seeks to bring the listener into fullest union with the Father, the Son, and the Holy Spirit. At the Last Supper, Jesus speaks of this union that is brought about through the power of the Holy Spirit:

"I have much more to tell you, but you cannot bear it now. But when he comes, the Spirit of truth, he will guide you to all truth. He will not speak on his own, but he will speak what he hears, and will declare to you the things that are coming. He will glorify me, because he will take from what is mine and declare it to you. Everything that the Father has is mine; for this reason I told you that he will take from what is mine and declare it to you" (Jn 16:12–15).

Like the previous two stages of faith, this third stage has two constitutive elements: first, the believer seeks to have a more profound understanding of the mystery that is being revealed, and, second, he seeks to participate in the mystery in all its fullness. Didascalia nourishes those Christians already mature in faith whom God is calling to a fullness of relationship. It is geared ultimately to fostering nothing less than what has classically been known as mystical union.

In the Letter to the Ephesians, Paul offers a prayer that this union might be accomplished:

"That he [the Father] may grant you in accord with the riches of his glory to be strengthened with power through his Spirit in the inner self, and that Christ may dwell in your hearts through faith; that you, rooted and grounded in love, may have strength to comprehend with all the holy ones what is the breadth and length and height and depth, and to know the love of Christ that surpasses knowledge, so that you may be filled with all the fullness of God" (Eph 3:16–19).

Perhaps the fact that the term is not a familiar one today is symptomatic of the need for more didascalic preaching. Although at present it most commonly occurs on retreats and in religious communities, didascalia should be a regular part of parish preaching because it contributes to the ordinary Christian community's development in faith. Because we human beings can never put limits on what God may will to accomplish in the lives of his children, we cannot say any Christian is not called to mystical union. Since didascalic preaching is an essential means by which this union is accomplished, it can be neither infrequent nor limited to special occasions or elite groups.

Furthermore, since it is not possible to be a true mystic in love with God without being in love with our fellow human beings, the mystic today is called to become involved in social expressions of the gospel teachings. Thus, the preaching of the "social gospel" is a significant, indeed essential, aspect of didascalic preaching.

The Letter of James stresses that faith necessarily and of itself, as it were, finds expression in action:

"Who among you is wise and understanding? Let him show his works by a good life in the humility that comes from wisdom. But the wisdom from above is first of all pure, then peaceable, gentle, compliant, full of mercy and good fruits, without inconstancy or insincerity. And the fruit of righteousness is sown in peace for those who cultivate peace" (Jas 3:13,17,18).

To implement the teachings of Christ in specific programs of political and social action requires great strength and great stamina—more than the human being alone has. Social action is a fruit of grace brought by the hearing of the word; it is the fruit of deep union with Christ. If many who are involved in social expressions of the gospel become frustrated and leave the arena of battle after relatively short periods of time, it is due, perhaps, to the fact that their union with Christ was not deep enough to bear the hardships of implementing the gospel. Paul wrote about the sufferings the preacher may face:

"Now I rejoice in my sufferings for your sake, and in my flesh I am filling up what is lacking in the afflictions of Christ on behalf of his body, which is the church, of which I am a minister in accordance with God's stewardship given to me to bring to completion for you the word of God, the mystery hidden from ages and from generations past. But now it has been manifested to his holy ones, to whom God chose to make known the riches of the glory of this mystery among the Gentiles; it is Christ in you, the hope of glory. It is he whom we proclaim, admonishing everyone and teaching everyone with all wisdom, that we may present everyone perfect in Christ. For this I labor and struggle, in accord with the exercise of his power working within me" (Col 1:24–29).

THE LITURGICAL HOMILY

We should note at this point that the liturgical homily is not a distinct kind of preaching in the sense we have been explaining. Rather "liturgical homily" describes the structure for preaching that takes place in liturgical celebrations. The liturgical homily should be capable of reaching persons who are living in various stages of faith development.

For example, marriage and funeral liturgies are excellent opportunities to preach to the unevangelized because, frequently, the guests at both have not seen the inside of a church for years, if at all. Baptisms are effective moments for catechizing young parents. Anointings of the sick enable the preacher to touch the hearts of those affected by the crisis and bring them into more intimate union with the Lord. And, of course, the eucharistic congregation on Sunday is made up the entire spectrum of the Christian community, including the nonbeliever who is Catholic in name only.

In the chapters that follow, we will describe how these kinds of preaching foster the varieties of faith experience.

NOTES

1. As we have noted previously, there is a complexity of causality to the act of faith. Always the actual assent of the human will to what God reveals is dependent on a direct internal movement of grace by the Holy Spirit. At the same time, external graces, such as Scripture and preaching, are real causes of faith in that they specify the object to which the will assents. See Note 1 in Chapter One.

2. Cf. Hoge, *Converts, Dropouts, Returnees* (New York: Pilgrim Press, 1981), p. 85.

3. Rev. Alvin Illig, writing in *Evangelization and Initiation* (Washington, DC: The Paulist National Catholic Evangelization Association), January/February, 1986.

4. Kevin Perrotta, "Are the Baby-Boomers Coming Back to Church?" in *Pastoral Review*, Vol. 11, No. 9 (April, 1987).

5. See "didaskalia" in *Theological Dictionary of the New Testament*, ed. by Gerhard Kittel, tr. by Geoffrey W. Bromiley (Grand Rapids, MI: Wm. B. Eerdmans Publishing Company, 1964), Vol II, p. 160.

Chapter Six

Evangelization

Perhaps nowhere do we see more clearly the absolute freedom, power, and love of God than when he calls members of our human race to union with himself through faith. We see God's freedom because, as we have emphasized from the beginning, faith is an absolutely free gift of God, a grace he gives to those to whom he wills to give it simply because he wills to do so. Faith is not something we are owed or that we can deserve, merit or earn. We can only accept it and enjoy the change in life faith brings.

God's power is manifest in faith because only God can change our hearts and deliver us from all its evils that hold us in bondage. He does this by making us want to be good and holy. Through the prophet Ezechiel the Lord God described what he will do when we believe:

"I will sprinkle clean water upon you to cleanse you from all your impurities, and from all your idols I will cleanse you. I will give you a new heart and place a new spirit within you, taking from your bodies your stony hearts and giving you natural hearts. I will put my spirit within you and make you live by my statutes, careful to observe my decrees" (Ez 36:25–27).

This change in the way we live will not be instantaneous and may take a long time, down a long road, filled with suffering, but it will be a road that leads to eternal life. Paul describes the process:

"Affliction produces assurance, and endurance, proven character, and proven character, hope, and hope does not disappoint, because the love of God has been poured out into our hearts through the holy Spirit that has been given to us" (Rom 5:3–5).

God's love is shown in the conversion process because his love is the reason why he calls us to himself and forgives our sins. The greatest evidence of his love is the fact that Christ died for us and through his death and resurrection unites us to his Father:

"God proves his love for us in that while we were still sinners Christ died for us. How much more then, since we are now justified by his blood, will we be saved through him from the wrath. Indeed, if, while we were enemies, we were reconciled to God through the death of his Son, how much more, once reconciled, will we be saved by his life" (Rom 5:8–10).

Jesus Christ is God's love-made-flesh. He is the channel of all God's graces to the world because Jesus and the Father are one.[1]

THE COMPLEXITY OF CONVERSION: SCRIPTURE

Conversion, the goal of evangelization, starts when Jesus calls the convert to faith and gives him both the desire and the power to respond to the call. As Jesus said: "It was not you who chose me, but I who chose you" (Jn 15:16).

The Acts of the Apostles, the inspired story of the earliest converts to Christianity, reflects the diversity of ways God called them to conversion and the variety of inspired preachings that led to it. The first great conversion recorded in the Acts took place as the result of Peter's preaching. Peter and the other apostles had been meeting when they heard the loud noise of a powerful wind throughout the house. So great was the noise that the people outside in the street heard it.

131

A crowd began to collect outside the place where the apostles were. Then the people heard the apostles speaking many different languages. While some of the men of Jerusalem put the whole thing down to drunkenness, Peter demonstrated that what had happened was the result of the outpouring of the Holy Spirit, the fulfillment of prophecy and the effect of the ministry, death, and resurrection of Jesus. And three thousand believed.[2]

The healing of a lame man by Peter and John was another occasion for a sermon by Peter in which he stressed again the fulfillment of prophecy.[3] When Peter raised Tabitha from the dead, "This became known all over Joppa, and many came to believe in the Lord" (Acts 9:42).

The story of the conversion of the Ethiopian eunuch offers a different experience of conversion. In this story, the eunuch has just completed a pilgrimage to Jerusalem. Although he is reading and pondering the Scriptures, he is not able to penetrate their meaning. Then the Holy Spirit sends Philip to him. Philip explains that the passage the eunuch is reading from Isaiah is a prophecy of Christ's passion and death. When the eunuch hears what that has accomplished, he asks for baptism so he can enter into the mystery of Christ. After baptism, he goes on his way rejoicing.[4]

Cornelius, the Roman centurion, is another non-Jew who is seeking union with God. He is a devout man who has been offering prayers and alms; he had also led his entire household into God-fearing ways. As a result of a vision, he summons Peter, who responds to Cornelius' call and explains to him the meaning of the Good News. Immediately, there is an outpouring of the Holy Spirit, and Cornelius and his household see where all their search has been leading them. Their trust in God is given new strength by their hearing of his word, and their minds are enlightened by God's truth. Their growing faith and understanding culminate in their baptism.

A sudden and blinding vision is the outstanding feature of Paul's conversion, although there are indications that Paul had been previously in spiritual turmoil. He had, after all, seen Stephen stoned, a particularly cruel, bloody, and drawn-out death. Paul had approved of the stoning. Furthermore, Paul took a very active part in the persecution of the earliest Christians, both men and women. While he was engaged in these activities, he must have become increasingly familiar with the basic tenets of the Christian faith that drove the "followers of the Way" to such zealous witness. He must also have reflected on the person of Jesus. Thus, Jesus had only to identify himself by name for Paul to recognize him and to quickly and wholeheartedly submit: "What am I to do, Lord?"

While the Lord Jesus himself brought Paul into the faith, immediately upon his conversion, the Lord sent him to the Church in Antioch to "be told what you must do" (Acts 9:1–19).

Paul preached mainly in the synagogues of the Jews until he had established his own churches. There, Paul, like Peter, stressed the fulfillment of prophecy— a rather widespread form of preaching in the early Church. Although Paul performed miracles that did lead people to the Lord, Acts does not emphasize them.

One of the most unusual approaches to conversion that Paul took was in his talk to the Greeks in Athens. Here he stressed the use of reason in coming to a knowledge of "the unknown God." Scripture indicates that although most did not accept his message, Paul's words brought two significant and influential early

Christians into the faith: Dionysius, the Areopagite, and Damaris.[5]

Every preaching event, then, has immeasurable, unknown, yet, nevertheless, great consequences, according to the intention of God who "wills everyone to be saved and to come to knowledge of the truth" (1 Tm 2:4).

THE DIVERSITY OF EXPERIENCE

People have always come to God in different ways. The history of the Christian Church is filled with the stories of great saints who followed markedly different paths in arriving at union with God. Think of St. Augustine's long and difficult conversion, for example. He was the child of God begotten by St. Monica's tears. How different from St. Paul's conversion as recounted in Acts.

Today people still come to God by distinctive routes. Read the stories of Thomas Merton, C. S. Lewis, Avery Dulles, and Emilie Griffin. Each story is unique, yet all have arrived at the same blessed relationship with their loving Father.

While conversion demands a turning away from sin and a definitive turning to God, the recognition of one's sinfulness may not be the first step in conversion. A desire to flee what has been perceived as a pursuer or adversary has marked the beginning of more than one convert's journey to faith. Jeremiah's reaction to his call to prophesy is a classic example of fleeing God. He complains:

"Whenever I speak, I must cry out,
    violence and outrage is my message;
The word of the LORD has brought me
    derision and reproach all the day.
I say to myself, I will not mention him,
    I will speak in his name no more.

But then it becomes like fire burning in my heart,
  imprisoned in my bones;
I grow weary holding it in,
  I cannot endure it.

Cursed be the day
  on which I was born!
May the day my mother gave me birth
  never be blessed!" (Jer 20:8,9,14)

Jeremiah was not the eager Isaiah who said:
"Then I heard the voice of the Lord saying, 'Whom
shall I send? Who will go for us?' 'Here I am,' I said;
'send me!' " (Is 6:8)

Francis Thompson in his moving poem, *The Hound of
Heaven*, has also captured that experience of flight in
the opening stanza:

"I fled Him, down the nights and down the days;
  I fled Him, down the arches of the years;
I fled Him, down the labyrinthine ways
Of my own mind; and in the midst of tears
I hid from Him."[6]

The recollections of the converts themselves seem to
indicate that the very first movement in the conversion experience is a sense of "being involved" (a deliberately vague term) in some way with a Superior Being. C. S. Lewis speaks of his early call to faith as
being in a struggle with an Adversary. Avery Dulles
saw an ordinary tree on the bank of the Charles River
in a new light and recognized that a Person must have
designed it and crafted it.

A DEFINITION OF CONVERSION

From the testimonies of converts both in the Bible and
outside it, we can define conversion as a complex inner process of profound change, under the impetus of
God's grace both internal and external, that results in

135

the reshaping of one's life because of the acquiring of a new mentality and outlook.

The conversion experience, whatever form it takes, results in a new set of values to live by, which is expressed by the biblical concepts of the "new heart" (Ez 36:26), the "new creation" (2 Cor 5:17), the "new person" (Eph 2:15), and the "new self" (Eph 4:24). Conversion culminates in new understanding—the wisdom of the Cross—and it confers a new power to love in accord with that new wisdom. It is the "Way" (Acts 9:2).

In the beginning stages, however, that new power to love may be very feeble and can be better expressed by saying that the convert at least "wants" to love. It may take quite some time and a great deal of personal discipline before the believer is actually able to act in even close approximation to his new ideals.

Conversion, when all is said and done, is the intellectual, emotional, and experiential discovery of meaning. The reason why conversion accounts have about them an air of the miraculous is because the new understandings seem so utterly gratuitous and unmerited to the convert. The insights that faith brings, perhaps over a long period of time, give a new appreciation of all reality as the handiwork of a loving God. As a result, the convert is more and more able to recognize the Creator's wisdom in the things he has made and is able to see God's personal guidance of himself in all the events of his life. As a result, the convert feels at one with all creation; he experiences a sense of inner and outer harmony with nature and is at peace.

THE THEOCENTRICITY OF THE CONVERSION EXPERIENCE

Roman Catholic conversion preaching is always Trinitarian and not just Christocentric. Both preaching and the sacramental life are intended to lead the believer into a new and deeper relationship with the Triune God: Father, Son, and Holy Spirit—not just with Jesus. The Church's liturgies reflect this understanding. The central liturgy of the Church, the Holy Sacrifice of the Mass, is addressed to the Father as the object of appeal and praise. Eucharistic Prayer I, the most ancient of the anaphoras used by the Church today, for example, begins:

"We come to you, Father, with praise and thanksgiving, through Jesus Christ your Son. Through him we ask you to accept and bless these gifts we offer you in sacrifice."

The basis for the Church's teaching is, of course, Scripture. When his disciples asked Jesus to teach them to pray, he taught them to say: "Our Father in heaven" (Mt 6:9; cf. Lk 11:2). During the last supper, as recounted in the Gospel of John, Jesus again teaches his disciples to pray directly to the Father:

"Amen, amen, I say to you, whatever you ask the Father in my name he will give you. . . . On that day you will ask in my name, and I do not tell you that I will ask the Father for you. For the Father himself loves you, because you have loved me and have come to believe that I came from God" (Jn 16:23–27).

Although in the Bible Jesus taught us to pray to the Father, the Church's understanding of the Trinity as it is expressed in its creeds, especially the Nicene Creed, is a postbiblical development of Christianity. Our present and commonly accepted understanding of the Trinity did not reach maturity and its final form until the First Ecumenical Council at Constantinople in 381 A.D., almost 350 years after the writing of the New Testament by the Church.

Trinitarianism begins with the acknowledgment of the unique position of God the Father. All prayers are addressed to him as the Principle of being, related to the other Persons of the Trinity insofar as they proceed from him, although the Father himself proceeds from no other. This is not to say that the Father is the cause of the Son or the Holy Spirit. All three Persons are uncaused. The Father, however, is the one from whom the others proceed as from a Principle.

The second aspect of Trinitarianism is the redemptive work of the Second Person of the Blessed Trinity, the Word. He was made flesh and dwelt among us as Jesus, the Christ. The redemptive work of the Second Person continues today in the active presence and powerful touch of the Risen Jesus in the sacraments of his Church. As Risen Head of his body, the Church, Jesus is present to the faithful through the reading of the Scriptures and the celebration of the sacraments. The sacramental life of the Church, in fact, is essential to the life and growth of believers. This is reflected in the teaching of the Gospel of John regarding the Eucharist, the central sacrament of Christianity. The gospel attributes to Jesus himself the command to celebrate the Eucharist:

"Amen, amen, I say to you, unless you eat the flesh of the Son of Man and drink his blood, you do not have life within you" (Jn 6:53).

Since Trinitarianism is not just an ideology, but an actual communication of the Godhead with human beings today, it requires an ecclesial system that makes it possible for the living Body of Christ, the Church to celebrate the sacraments. Hence, Pope, bishops, priests, and deacons are essential for both the preservation of right teaching and continuation of the sacramental channeling of Jesus' grace.

The Holy Spirit's life-giving activity, promised in the gospels and recorded in the Acts of the Apostles is more fully explained in the Church's theological understanding of the biblical term *justification*.

"We know that all things work for good for those who love God, who are called according to his purpose. For those he foreknew he also predestined to be conformed to the image of his Son, so that he might be the firstborn among many brothers. And those whom he predestined he also called; and those he called he also justified; and those whom he justified he also glorified" (Rom 8:28–30).

When, under the impulse of divine grace a person puts his faith in Jesus, he undergoes an ontological, inward transformation from sinner to saint. There is a real infusion of sanctifying or transforming grace that removes sin and gives the believer the power to live virtuously, with a true interior goodness. Thus, by the power of God, the convert has become a true saint capable of doing good works, which are meritorious in the order of salvation. For this reason, St. Paul can write to the Philippians:

"For God is the one who, for his good purpose, works in you both to desire and to work" (Phil 2:13).

The Holy Spirit as the Principle of sanctification is an active presence in the life of the believer. The Holy Spirit brings about the New Creation to which Paul refers so frequently in his letters, especially in Romans 8. The Letter to the Ephesians sums it up:

"[There is] one body and one Spirit, as you were also called to the one hope of your call; one Lord, one faith, one baptism; one God and Father of all, who is over all and through all and in all" (Eph 4:3–6).

All of this theological understanding of Christian tradition reaches its summation in the "indwelling of the Blessed Trinity," a doctrine presented in many diverse forms over the centuries by a succession of Christian mystics with tireless enthusiasm. It is the ultimate development of Jesus' teaching in the Gospel of John:

"Whoever loves me will keep my word, and my Father will love him, and we will come to him and make our dwelling with him" (Jn 14:23).

THE DARKNESS OF CONVERSION

The initial conversion experience does not seem always to culminate in a moment of repentance and a calling out to be saved by Jesus. It does not always and immediately lead to a "decision for Christ" as the conversion ritual of the altar call expects. Such a decision, of course, may be made. Indeed, many testify that they made such a decision and can even identify the time and place they did so.

Nevertheless, for many converts to Christianity, the climactic moment of initial conversion is darker. That is, they make a decision without really knowing what the decision will lead to. It is a decision to put their entire life into the hands of him who demands absolutely everything of them. There can be no bargaining, no holding back, no reservations. The moment demands a complete and total act of self-giving and trust. Throughout the centuries, so many have described their moment of conversion as a leap of faith into darkness, but a darkness that holds the promise of eternal life.

C. S. Lewis in his memoirs of conversion, *Surprised by Joy*, describes the moment as he experienced on the top of a London bus.

"I felt myself being, there and then, given a free choice. I could open the door, or keep it shut; I could unbuckle the armor or keep it on. Neither choice was presented as a duty; no threat or promise was attached to either, though I knew that to open the door or to take off the corslet meant the incalculable. I chose to open. I say, 'I chose,' yet it did not really seem possible to do the opposite."[7]

A Lengthy Process of Change
The moment of darkness and the leap of faith are only the beginning of a lengthy, actually life-long, process of transformation as the consequence of a powerful movement of grace, personified in the Holy Spirit; the convert will undergo a continuing maturation for the rest of his life. The result of this transformation is growth in the knowledge of the One Who has called him into union with himself. Joined with growth in knowledge is a constant experience of the redemptive activity of Jesus' presence that enlightens the convert's heart and mind. Theological writers describe this transforming process as growth in the theological, intellectual and moral virtues. The Letter to the Ephesians exhorts all to growth:

"Living the truth in love, we should grow in every way into him who is the head, Christ, from whom the whole body, joined and held together by every supporting ligament, with the proper functioning of each part, brings about the body's growth and builds itself up in love" (Eph 4:15,16).

Growth is made possible by the Risen Jesus through the ministry of his Church.

In *A Testimonial to Grace*, Avery Dulles speaks of his hunger for union with Christ in his Church after his initial conversion:

"My ears were impatient to hear the sound of his voice saying through the lips of his appointed priest, 'Thy sins are forgiven thee.' My eyes cared to look upon naught else if they could not behold him in the Holy Eucharist. The very sense of touch craved to feel the trickling waters of baptism. The tongue was dry and the stomach empty with hunger to receive substantially the Bread of Life."[8]

Union with the Church

Not all appreciate the intimate union between Christ and his Church. Where the Church is, there is Jesus; where Jesus is, there is the Church. At the Last Supper, Jesus prayed to his Father for his disciples:

"As you sent me into the world, so I sent them into the world. And I consecrate myself for them, so that they also may be consecrated in truth.

"I pray not only for them, but also for those who will believe in me through their word, so that they may all be one, as you, Father, are in me and I in you, that they also may be in us, that the world may believe that you sent me" (Jn 17:18–21).

Ephesians 1:22,23 says that Jesus is the "head over all things to the church, which is his body." And Paul says in Colossians 1:18, "He is the head of the body, the church." And in Romans 12:5, Paul teaches, "We, though many, are one body in Christ and individually parts of one another."

While the scriptural teaching is very clear and the theological tradition is consistent that Christ and his Church form an indissoluble unity, contemporary Christian denominationalism tends to obscure the intimate identification of Christ with his Church. Furthermore, since Christ's Church is made up of sinners, evangelists must be prepared to have the sins of the sinners obscure the holiness of the body. Excesses of clericalism obscure the value of a stable, official leadership structure. Lazy leaders obscure the dynamic energy of God's people. Power-hungry pastors substitute their own will for God's. The list of abuses by the rich and powerful, as well as by the ordinary Christian, is centuries old, and the abuses were all condemned by the Prophet Hosea long before the coming of Christ:

"Hear the word of the LORD, O people of Israel,
   for the LORD has a grievance
   against the inhabitants of the land:
There is no fidelity, no mercy,
   no knowledge of God in the land.
False swearing, lying, murder, stealing
   and adultery!
in their lawlessness, bloodshed follows bloodshed.
. . . .
   with you is my grievance, O priests!
. . . .
My people perish for want of knowledge!"
(Hos 4:1 ff.)

While the faithful struggle against sinful influences in their lives and the life of the Church, sin and sinners will always be at work within the Church and its members. Therefore, when the evangelist teaches about the Church, he needs to distinguish between the sinful human beings who comprise it and the community that is holy through its union with Christ, a community that God has made the instrument of his saving action.

"Now, this holiness of the Church is unceasingly manifested, as it ought to be, through those fruits of grace that the Spirit produces in the faithful. It is expressed in multiple ways by those individuals who, in their walk of life, strive for the perfection of charity, and thereby help others to grow (*Lumen Gentium*, No. 39).

Evangelization clearly is easier in a parish where the pastor is loving, caring, and manifestly a good and holy man. Yet, evangelists can still preach the gospel with fruit to those seeking salvation in parishes led by pastors who may be selfish, narrow-minded, opinionated, and indifferent.

Paul ran into a similar problem when some of his fellow preachers preached Christ out of a sense of "rivalry and competition." However, he recognized that whatever the motive, the important thing is that Christ be proclaimed. He wrote:

"Some preach Christ from motives of envy and rivalry, others from good will. The latter act out of love, aware that I am here [in prison] for the defense of the gospel; the former proclaim Christ out of selfish ambition, not from pure motives, thinking that they will cause me trouble in my imprisonment. What difference does it make, as long as in every way, whether in pretense or in truth, Christ is being proclaimed? And in that I rejoice" (Phil 1:15–18).

The Risen Savior is united to his Church; he acts through his pilgrim Church on earth, even though his Church includes sinners who have not yet become saints.

The Qualities of Preaching That Can Lead to Conversion
Before all else, the evangelist must be humbly and constantly aware that the entire conversion process that brings an individual into union with Jesus is the result of the divine initiative in the life of the convert. The evangelist must be sensitive to the fact that the converts he makes are his "work in the Lord" (1 Cor 9:1), for it is God who is at work in the most basic, primitive, and essential way. The convert's ability to hear the preaching of the evangelist, whatever form that preaching takes, depends on a movement of grace in the convert's heart. So, too, the evangelist's ability to preach a message that will result in conversion is de-

pendent on the activity of the Holy Spirit in the preacher's life.

Because the preacher speaks from faith to beget faith, as has been previously explained, all evangelization demands the personal witness of the preacher. It is not sufficient to be knowledgeable about doctrinal propositions or moral law. When the evangelist proclaims the truths of the Christian faith his proclamation needs to flow from his own personal experience of faith. He preaches God's truth, which has become his own personal truth. In the case of the martyrs, their owning the truth led to their dying for Christ.

For example, in preaching on the authenticity of the Catholic Church as Christ's own Church, which surely must be done at some point, the evangelist cannot simply rattle off the four marks of Christ's Church and explain in some abstract and detached classroom manner how they are verified in the Roman Catholic Church today.

The effective evangelist draws upon his own experience of finding the verification for the Church as he lives out his faith in the Catholic community. The specific way he does this will depend on the creative way the individual evangelist is willing to "be there" for God and neighbor. Perhaps this is why the Lord has deemed to communicate his saving truth through a variety of preachers, since no one preacher can capture and communicate all of the mystery that is involved. The experienced truth of revelation gives power to his human word to reveal divine truth and, thereby, give birth to faith in the hearts of others.

There is a further dimension to witnessing. When the evangelist speaks out of a daily, living-faith experience, there is a greater likelihood of his communicating true insight into the meaning of life in Christ.

Insight, as we have seen, puts us in touch with the complexity of the human condition. Insight enables the evangelist to avoid the pitfalls of oversimplification.

Religious educators, on the other hand, might be prone to oversimplify the gospel message to make it easy for their students to understand. Nevertheless, the fact of the matter is the gospel message is not easy to understand (it is, after all, a mystery), and the meaning of life is not easy to understand. Whenever the message is oversimplified, it loses something of its truth; and when it loses something of its truth, it loses something of its credibility.

For example, when religion is taught to young children, it necessarily is taught in its most basic terms. If, however, the basic teaching is not developed and amplified over the years, the young adult will not be able to see its relevance to his present situation. In fact, he may find the earlier teaching so inadequate in meeting the needs of his more mature life that he will abandon the faith of his childhood. The failure to mature in the understanding of the truths of the gospel is the major reason so many leave the Church during their adolescent and young adult years.

If the communication of the gospel message should not be oversimplified, what should it be?

First, it should be expressed clearly. The evangelist should express the aspect of the gospel he seeks to communicate on any given occasion and to any given audience as clearly as possible, carefully delineating the scope and limits of his teaching, articulating his ideas logically and coherently, with emphasis on the fact that we are dealing with a mystery.

This principle applies to the evangelizing of the young and the very young as well as to the evangelizing of adults. It is easier for a person to accept the concept of mystery to begin with than to find out later that he has been told only the simplest facts and that they are not the whole story.

Second, the teaching has to be formulated in the evangelist's mind, and then it must be expressed in a way that will cause a resonance emotionally and psychologically in the hearer. The preacher is, after all, attempting to insert the kerygma into the life of another human being. The insertion, therefore, necessarily takes place in terms of what "makes the listener tick," rather than of what makes the preacher preach.

Making the communication relevant to the life, needs, and hurts of the listener is particularly important in preaching to convert. Here the preacher is not seeking a minor behavioral modification in the listener, but the transformation of a life.

Evangelization begins with the understanding that until now the convert has been living according to first principles that are not Christian. That is, he has had a mind set or mental attitude by which he judges all input he receives about reality. Perhaps it has been the principle "God does not exist." Now the evangelist tells him God does, in fact, exist, and God is the One who is calling to him from the void and darkness of his life. If all the convert's previous experience has convinced him God does not exist, something needs to happen to enable him to acquire the new principle of understanding and operation, "God exists."

The catalyst for change is emotion. These catalytic emotional experiences have been described vividly by those who report their conversion. They have occurred in a fleeting moment in a garden, by a river, in a church, on a bus. When they have happened, the entire being of the person starts to change, and the convert becomes free to accept the new intellectual understanding of his situation.

When, therefore, the evangelist seeks to communicate the truth of the gospel, he has to incorporate into his communication an appeal to emotion that will strike a responsive chord in the heart as well as the mind of his listener.[9] Christian evangelists are not just explaining doctrine or ideology. Through the articulation of revealed truth, they are instruments of God's uniting fellow human beings to the Father and Jesus. The Father and Jesus particularize their love for us through the Holy Spirit in the sacramental life of the Roman Catholic Church. In preaching to converts, therefore, evangelists reveal the Triune God as Persons who created, save, and love the convert.

STEPS IN PREACHING TO CONVERT

In preaching to convert, the evangelist must be aware of those needs, hurts, experiences, and attitudes of the potential convert that will cry out for the help and guidance of the gospel message in his life.

God speaks to us not only through the words of Scripture and the teaching of the Church; he speaks to us directly through all of our experiences, past and present. Through the things that happen to us, his loving hand has shaped us in the course of our entire life to be the person we are. Of course, in saying this, we are not attributing to God the evil twists that our own sins have caused. Nevertheless, even our sinfulness does not prevent God from acting in our lives to bring us to himself.

"But God, who is rich in mercy, because of the great love he had for us, even when we were dead in our transgressions, brought us to life with Christ (by grace you have been saved), and raised us up with him, and

148

seated us with him in the heavens in Christ Jesus" (Eph 2:4–6).

Conversion preaching therefore is designed to help the convert understand the meaning of his experiences as movements of grace bringing him into union with God. To be effective, the evangelist needs to know where the convert is standing now in relation to the Lord. The potential convert may not be conscious of an explicit relationship to God, yet such a relationship exists.

To clarify this already existing relationship, the evangelist should explore what experiences the convert is having that cause him to reflect on his present way of life. What events are presently happening to him that are moving him to seek new understanding about the meaning of life? Why does he need to experience new meaning? What is he looking for?

The occasions for the reexamination of life are many: it may be a severe crisis or tragedy, either personal or in the family, that leads to the question, "Why," or perhaps more significantly, "Why me?" It may be a feeling of powerlessness and lack of personal control. Sometimes it is disgust with one's present way of life, an awareness of being steeped in evil that is the result of one's own sinfulness. It could be loneliness, a major problem today, or such a simple thing as curiosity. Yet, all of these experiences are graced moments in the life of the convert of any age and part of God's call to more intimate union with him.[10]

This familiarity with the needs and experiences of the convert is why most adult conversions to Roman Catholicism take place because of intermarriage with a Catholic and are facilitated by a spouse, relative, or priest.[11]

Once the evangelist identifies, under the impulse of grace, the situation of the convert, he can begin to show the convert how God is bringing him close to himself. For example, today many people are lonely. More and more they come from small families. Perhaps they have been divorced; with increasing frequency, they are the children of divorced parents. They find themselves at a loss in a world that is complicated and confusing, and they do not feel competent to deal with the many issues of their lives. Afraid to enter into interpersonal relationships, they cut themselves off from others. They indulge in activities that isolate instead of unify. The end result is a feeling of intense loneliness, abandonment, and uselessness. Many of the case histories of people, young and old, who have committed suicide reflect these feelings and experiences.

On the positive side, such experiences, painful as they are, provide opportunities for the sensitive evangelist to witness to God's personal love for each of us and his constant presence to all of us. Certainly that is a major theme of the both the Old and New Testaments. God calls to us to deliver us from our personal isolation and loneliness into the fellowship of the Holy Spirit by living in the Christian community. This practical implementation of the teaching of Ephesians 1:3–14 is an effective way of delivering the lonely from their isolation and leading them into the promised kingdom.

CONVERSION IS FOR THE YOUNG

This transformation of life and outlook that brings the convert to God happens most often to the young. It can and does happen at any age, of course, but Jesus was in his late twenties and early thirties when he began to preach, and many of the disciples he attracted were young. In our own day, Avery Dulles was an undergraduate at Harvard when he became a Christian; Thomas Merton was in his early twenties. And was it not C. S. Lewis who said that most of us had our most important thoughts before the age of fourteen?

In other words, since we human beings seek the meaning of our lives when we are young, evangelizers should make an effort to gear their preaching to the interests and experiences of young people. This will be difficult for preachers who have distanced themselves from the experience of the young and in so doing have lost touch with their world. Therefore, the preacher who seeks to convert must either reestablish communality with young people or turn the task of evangelization to those who are in daily touch with a youthful world.

NOTES

1. John 10:30.

2. Acts 2:1–41.

3. Acts 3:1–26.

4. Acts 8:26–40.

5. Acts 17:16–34.

6. Francis Thompson, *The Hound of Heaven* (New York: Dodd, Mead & Co., 1926).

7. C. S. Lewis, *Surprised by Joy: The Shape of My Life* (New York: Harcourt, Brace and World, 1955), p. 224.

8. Avery Dulles, *A Testimonial to Grace* (New York: Sheed and Ward, 1946), p. 105.

9. The classic Greek and Latin rhetoricians can be guides here because they show how to use oratory to remove emotional blocks to the communication of their message.

10. Since there is evidence that children in the fourth, fifth, and sixth grades are already beginning their search for meaning, evangelists who are ministering to children of this age will have to adapt the exploration of life values and experiences to the comprehension of this age group.

11. Hoge, *Converts, Dropouts, Returnees* (New York: Pilgrim Press, 1981), p. 33.

Chapter Seven

Catechesis

The goal of catechesis is the building up of a personal relationship to Jesus Christ so that the convert can enter more fully into the mystery of salvation first revealed to him through evangelization. A fundamental characteristic of this relationship as a member of the People of God is a need to praise God for the greatness of the gift he has bestowed on his People.

"You are a 'chosen race, a royal priesthood, a holy nation, a people of his own, so that you may announce the praises' of the one who called you out of darkness into his wonderful light" (1 Pt 2:9).

Since the convert experiences, as so many attest, an exciting sense of joy and freedom, the focus of catechesis is to stabilize that faith experience into a way of life by providing deeper penetration into the meaning of the word of God. As we saw, evangelization reveals to the convert the significance of his life as one who has been chosen. It enables him to recognize the divine purpose in the events that led the new believer into explicit union with Jesus. Psalm 139 beautifully describes the experience of those who see God's hand at work in their lives:

"Truly you have formed my inmost being;
    you knit me in my mother's womb.
I give you thanks that I am fearfully,
        wonderfully made;
    wonderful are your works.

Your eyes have seen my actions;
  in your book they are all written;
  my days were limited before one of them existed.
How weighty are your designs, O God;
  how vast the sum of them!" (Ps 139:13–14,16–17).

Catechesis continues the transformation begun during the initial conversion by building on the truths that were accepted in faith. The basic truths of the Christian creed, once accepted, are the solid foundation for a more penetrating exploration of God's revelation, leading ultimately to glorification.

"We know that all things work for good for those who love God, who are called according to his purpose. For those whom he foreknew he also predestined to be conformed to the image of his Son, so that he might be the firstborn among many brothers. And those whom he predestined he also called; and those he called he also justified; and those he justified he also glorified" (Rom 8:28–30).

Much of this exploration has to be done in a systematic manner because of the rational nature of the human mind. The fruits of theological reflection under the guidance of the Church, therefore, need to be communicated to converts in a way that enables them to see the interconnection between the truths themselves as well as the relevancy of those truths to daily life.

Nevertheless, catechesis is more than the systematic imparting of knowledge of revelation, as important as that is. To grow in the mystery of Christ to the point of glory, we who are already believers need a continual inner empowering by which we can both understand revelation and, at the same time, experience what the revelation means for our personal existence in a community of faith.

Catechetical preaching, then, has a two-fold thrust: first, it shows how a life of praise and thanksgiving can be most completely expressed in accord with God's will; second, it communicates the power to accomplish what one has been called to.

Consequently, the goal of catechesis is not merely information about God, Jesus, the Church, or religion. The goal is not simply to be able to list the moral imperatives of religious observance; it is not just the memorization of certain prayers or the awareness of religious customs and practices. It is not learning how to attend to Mass or say the rosary, although all of these things have a legitimate place in catechesis. Pope John Paul II, in his *Apostolic Exhortation on Catechesis in Our Time*, defines the goal of catechesis:

"The definitive aim of catechesis is to put people not only in touch but in communion, in intimacy, with Jesus Christ: only he can lead us to the love of the Father in the Spirit and make us share in the life of the Holy Trinity."[1]

Catechesis, whether in classrooms, study groups, Bible classes or church, generates in the hearers of the word of God, no matter how old or young they are, deeper trust in Jesus. It enables them to recognize and appreciate what God is doing in their lives now through the gifts he has given them. As Pope John Paul II says in the same document: "This teaching is not a body of abstract truths. It is the communication of the living mystery of God" (No. 7).

When catechetical preaching is effective, the believer will want to intensify his experience of the mystery of faith, Christ's presence in his life. Having heard the word, he wants to conscientiously prepare himself to be sensitive to God's movements and, thus, be assured of the life of glory yet to be revealed.

Above all, catechesis leads to holiness. Freed from his sins by the blood of Christ, the believer finds new life and peace through the taking of the word of God into his heart and the living out of his life in praise and thanksgiving. Catechesis motivates the believer to become a better disciple of the Lord and shows the ways to do it.

In order for catechetical preaching to bear fruit, however, the listener must first believe in Jesus. That is, he must have an initial relationship with Jesus that is founded on faith and trust. Catechesis nourishes that faith, but it does not give birth to it; that is the task of evangelization.

Of the many elements that comprise catechesis, both in terms of its content and methodology, two elements are essential: (1) the ongoing proclamation of the word of God and (2) the personal witness of the catechetical preacher. Although the need for these is being constantly reaffirmed by the Church, they are still not explicit requirements in those catechetical programs that are experiencing difficulty in attracting and holding participants.

A BIBLICAL MENTALITY

The Letter to Timothy recognizes that much of the weakness of religious practice is because Christians are neglecting the Scriptures; consequently, it makes a very specific appeal for Christians to read them.

"[The people in the last days] make a pretense of religion but deny its power. Reject them. . . . But you remain faithful to what you have learned and believed, because you know from whom you learned it, and that from infancy you have known the sacred scriptures, which are capable of giving you wisdom for salvation through faith in Christ Jesus. All scripture is inspired by God and is useful for teaching, for refutation, for correction, and for training in righteousness, so that one who belongs to God may be competent, equipped for every good work" (2 Tm 3:5,14–17).

Since faith comes from hearing the word of God,[2] obviously the word of God is essential to its growth. The *Dogmatic Constitution on Divine Revelation* concludes:

"Through the reading and study of the sacred books, let 'the word of the Lord run and be glorified' (2 Thes 3:1) and let the treasure of revelation entrusted to the Church increasingly fill the hearts of men. Just as the life of the Church grows through the persistent participation in the Eucharistic mystery, so we may hope for a new surge of spiritual vitality from intensified veneration for God's word, which 'lasts forever' " (No. 26).

Yet, in spite of its importance, many catechetical preaching programs do not foster a biblical mentality that encourages the individual Christian to pursue for himself more thorough reflection on the word of God.

For example, until recently Latin was an essential ingredient of an advanced Catholic education because the Church's worship was done in that language and its theological tradition was couched in it. Today, because Latin is no longer required for either worship or theological courses (it remains desirable for the more profound study of theology, of course), it has been dropped from the required curriculum in Catholic schools.

The Old Testament was originally written in Hebrew and the New Testament in Greek. Consequently, in spite of excellent translations that are easily available today, at least a rudimentary knowledge of those languages is as essential for serious study of the Bible as Latin used to be for the study and practice of Catholicism. Since the word of God is at the center of the

Church's teaching, catechetical programs should, if not require, at least make available the basics of Greek and Hebrew at the appropriate age levels. Thus, catechetical programs should say, in effect: "The Scriptures are so important that you should devote some of your time to learning the languages in which they were written." In addition, those being catechized should receive instruction in the cultures and civilizations of biblical time.

The understanding of the sacred author's milieu is important for the reader to be able to determine the literary forms the author uses to communicate. When the reader can recognize the difference between prose and poetry or myth and history or narrative and letter, he will be in a better position to perceive the author's intention and, therefore, he will be better able to grasp the truth the sacred writer is asserting. This principle is espoused with special clarity in the *Dogmatic Constitution on Divine Revelation*:

"Those who search out the intention of the sacred writer must, among other things, have regard for 'literary forms.' For truth is proposed and expressed in a variety of ways, depending on whether a text is history of one kind or another, or whether its form is that of prophecy, poetry, or some other type of speech. The interpreter must investigate what meaning the sacred writer intended to express and actually expressed in particular circumstances as he used contemporary literary forms in accordance with the situation of his own time and culture. From the correct understanding of what the sacred author wanted to assert, due attention must be paid to the customary and characteristic styles of perceiving, speaking, and narrating which prevailed at the time of the sacred writer, and to the customs men normally followed at that period in their everyday dealings with one another" (No. 12).

More recent developments in biblical criticism are insisting that while the author's intention is of great importance, the response of the reader to what has been written is also of great significance. Thus, there is an increasing interest among biblical scholars in "reader-response" criticism, especially as it casts light on the development of the canon of Scripture and the use the Church has made of the sacred writings in the past. As a result, "The approach of reader-response criticism has a great deal of meaning for how the Scriptures, in general, function in the Church today."[3]

By teaching how the Church contributes to the meaning of the Bible by the use it makes of it, catechetical preachers will be answering many of the problems raised by Fundamentalism. The Reverend Jerry Falwell, a leading exponent of Fundamentalism says;

"A Fundamentalist is one who believes the Bible to be verbally inspired by the Holy Spirit and, therefore, inerrant and absolutely infallible."[4]

For the Fundamentalist, the Bible speaks for itself; it requires no Church for interpreting it. Any Bible-believing Christian can simply pick up the Book and begin to read and find in its written words all the answers needed for a life of faith.

Such an approach fails to take into account the human element in the Bible and results in a literalism that eventually pits the Bible against science and common sense, as the controversy over evolution attests.

In short, with the development of a truly biblical mentality, familiarity with the development of revelation and doctrine in the past, as evidenced in the Bible itself, will show how the events of history have been channels of grace to God's people. God's grace continues to come to his people today through the Church. Thus, when an enlightened appreciation of the Bible is active, religious education is more than intellectual exercises in questions and answers, ideological subtleties, and moral imperatives. Formation in religion is the study, exploration, and experience of God's active ways with human beings in all ages.

Exploring the Ways of God
Here is only one example out of many that might be cited of how doctrine has developed in salvation history. The "Ten Commandments" are not a collection of abstract moral injunctions, fixed in stone in a single blinding moment on a mountain top in the distant past. They are the result of the Israelites' consciousness of their peculiar relationship to the Creator of all things as his chosen people. The moral values the Commandments enjoined upon this people underwent modification as lived experiences in subsequent generations as the great prophets applied the moral teachings of God's holiness to new situations. Indeed, many of the events that they endured were seen as punishment for the people's failure to live according to the teaching of "The Law."

For Christians, on the other hand, while the Ten Commandments have never lost their basic force as injunctions to holiness, they are only the minimum requirements for union with Jesus because the gospel calls and empowers the chosen people of today to a higher experience of love than the Ten Commandments demand. In Matthew, Chapter 5, Jesus reveals how much more he expects of his disciples than the Ten Commandments require: the injunction not to kill is replaced by a demand for reconciliation; prohibition of adultery is superceded by a call for purity. In other words, the necessity of love that was only implicitly revealed in the great event with Moses becomes the explicit fundament of the God's relation to his chosen people in Jesus Christ.

Catechists today continue this process of development by adapting the revealed truths to the new situations the People of God are encountering as a result of changes in historical circumstances. Pope John Paul II, in his encyclical letter of November 30, 1980, *Rich in Mercy*, recognized that in contemporary society there is a great awareness of the need for justice, especially social justice. Yet for all the great virtue of the sensitivity to the demands of justice, there is a concomittant rejection of human and divine mercy. He writes:

"The word and the concept of 'mercy' seem to cause uneasiness in man, who, thanks to the enormous development of science and technology never before known in history, has become the master of the earth and has subdued and dominated it. This dominion over the earth, sometimes understood in a one-sided and superficial way, seems to leave no room for mercy" (No. 2).[5]

The changed circumstances, which are obscuring the active presence of God in human life, demand that the Church, like the prophets of old, through her preachers, especially perhaps her catechists, develop the doctrine of mercy by adapting the perennial message of Christianity to meet the needs of our times. Pope John Paul II writes:

"In the name of Jesus Christ crucified and risen, in the spirit of his messianic mission, enduring in the history of humanity, we raise our voices and pray that the love which is in the Father may once again be revealed at this stage of history, and that, through the work of the Son and the Holy Spirit, it may be shown to be present in our modern world and to be more powerful than evil: more powerful than sin and death. . . . No matter how strong the resistance of human history may be, no matter how great the denial of God in the human world, so much the greater must be the church's closeness to that mystery which, hidden for centuries in God, was then truly shared with man, in time, through Jesus Christ" (No. 15).

The richness the Scriptures offer to Catholics has been neglected because a sacramental rather than biblical mentality permeates catechetical preaching as educational programs focus on preparing the young for the reception of the sacraments. And, of course, sacramental preparation is necessary. Nevertheless, faith must be present before the sacraments can produce fruit in terms of holiness of life and witness to the world, *ex opere operato.*

"The sacred liturgy does not exhaust the entire activity of the Church. Before men can come to the liturgy, they must be called to faith and to conversion. . . . To believers also the Church must ever preach faith and repentance. She must prepare them for the sacraments, teach them to observe all that Christ has commanded, and win them to all the works of charity, piety and the apostolate. For all these activities make it clear that Christ's faithful, though not of this world, are the light of the world and give glory to the Father in the sight of men" (*Constitution on the Sacred Liturgy,* No. 9).

All too often, it seems, those who are "prepared" for confirmation are prepared only to participate in the confirmation ritual, so that once the rite has been completed they no longer participate in the life of the Church.

While sacramental preparation clearly has a necessary place in Catholic formation, the word of God holds the central and most basic place in the handing on of the faith. In making the above observations, we do no more than specify what Pope John Paul II wrote in his *Exhortation on Catechesis in Our Time,* Numbers 26 and 27:

"The one message—the Good News of salvation—that has been heard once or hundreds of times and has been accepted with the heart, is in catechesis probed unceasingly by reflection and systematic study, by awareness of its repercussions on one's personal life—an awareness calling for ever greater commitment—and by inserting it into an organic and harmonious whole, namely Christian living in society and the world. Catechesis will always draw its content from the living source of the word of God transmitted in Tradition and the Scriptures. . . . To speak of Tradition and Scripture as the source of catechesis is to draw attention to the fact that catechesis must be impregnated and penetrated by the thought, the spirit and the outlook of the Bible and the Gospels through assiduous contact with the texts themselves; but it is also a reminder that catechesis will be all the richer and more effective for reading the texts with the intelligence and the heart of the Church and for drawing inspiration from the 2,000 years of the Church's reflection and life."

In the same year, 1979, Pope John Paul II applied the above understanding of the importance of a biblical mentality to advanced scholarship in his October address to the Presidents of Catholic Colleges and Universities at a convocation at The Catholic University of America:

"True theological scholarship and teaching cannot exist and be fruitful without seeking its inspiration and its source in the word of God as contained in Sacred Scripture and in the Sacred Tradition of the Church as interpreted by the authentic Magisterium throughout history."

A biblical mentality enthrones the Bible in places of honor in the Church, the school and the homes. Given Catholicism's sacramentalism and consequent high regard for the value of symbols, the Bible needs to be displayed for veneration in the church. A true biblical mentality would seem to demand that all adults and children in a Catholic parish have their own Bibles, which they have been motivated to read.

The Bibles that the parish provides for young people to use in Catholic schools and religious education programs should be attractively bound and sturdily constructed. Even after much use, they should still be in good condition; if not, they should be withdrawn from use and replaced by new ones. Furthermore, catechists and their students should be taught to treat the Bible with respect and handle it with loving care, much like Americans treat their flag. These are the most effective ways of assuring that the entire community will recognize the Bible as a unique and important book.

A biblical mentality further demands a good biblical library. It should contain biblical research materials suitable to the age and faith levels of the entire parish. These materials should be available for use by all, and a parish staff person should be prepared to advise borrowers on the use of the materials. Finally, and perhaps most importantly, the parish staff should motivate all the people to actually make use of the resources provided.

PERSONAL WITNESS

We live in an age of professionalism, and the mentality that accompanies it greatly influences Church ministry today. Seminarians are required to take professional courses in counseling, hospital pastoral care, prison ministry, and the like. Upon completion of these intensive programs, they receive professional certification. In addition to certification, competency in pastoral ministry is being measured in terms of professional degrees with increasing frequency.

Directors of religious education expect their catechists to acquire professional credentials through participation in workshops, seminars and graduate degree programs. But overemphasis on professionalism does not result in a significant growth in the Church in the United States. Why?

There are some things one cannot do professionally. Parents cannot raise their family professionally but coldly; a mother does not care for her children professionally and abstractly. Neither an old woman nor a young boy dies professionally. One can die well or poorly, but not professionally. There is an art to loving, and some are better lovers than others. But no one can love professionally.

In the same way, no minister of the gospel, ordained or unordained, can preach professionally. Preaching, like loving, dying, raising a family, transcends the category of the merely "professional" because preaching calls on all of the resources of the Christian person— the total investment of his faith, his love and his experience of God and the mystery of Christ among us—to communicate the gospel message.

Now there is, without doubt, a skill to preaching. Effective preaching uses art that has to be learned and exercised, and that, at the same time, depends on a certain "natural" talent for the task. Nevertheless, at the core, preaching is more than skill, art, or natural talent. Preaching, as we have seen, is the oral expression of the person of faith's own insight into the meaning of divine revelation.

The inadequacy of professionalism with its emphasis on expertise at the expense of the personal in the preaching of the Good News has tremendous consequences for the parish community. To pass on the faith requires more than a professional director of religious education, competent teachers, and an organized curriculum. To pass on the faith, the parish community needs witnesses.

A parochial catechetical program, therefore, whether for children or adults first has to motivate faith-filled witnesses to preach catechetically; then it has to train them in the skills by which they become capable of doing it. No parish can assume its potential catechists are faith-filled witnesses. If there are cases where catechetical programs are not bearing rich fruit, the programs should be reexamined at each stage to see that all the elements necessary for effective catechetical preaching are present.

At the same time, sincere witnesses need to be trained to use the arts of catechetical preaching so that they do not just recount personal anecdotes even of a spiritual nature, but something of scriptural and theological substance in a coherent, even systematic, manner. In the light of their own experience of God, they must be trained to communicate insight into meaning in the way we have been describing. The two most recent Popes spoke directly to this issue.

Pope Paul VI, in *Evangelii Nuntiandi*, called for witnesses:

"Modern man listens more willingly to witnesses than to teachers, and if he does listen to teachers, it is because they are witnesses" (No. 41).

Pope John Paul II, in his general audience of August 29, 1979, called for insight:

"Catechesis cannot be limited simply to the communication of religious information. It must help to set alight in souls that light which is Christ. Such a light must illuminate effectively the entire path of human life."

166

Furthermore, the community Pope John Paul II described as a prerequisite for the communication of faith in a Catholic university applies with equal validity to the catechetical programs of parishes:

"A Catholic university must set up, among faculty and students, a real community which bears witness to a living and operative Christianity, a community where sincere commitment to scientific research and study goes together with a deep commitment to authentic Christian living."[6]

In other words, the quality of the spiritual, intellectual, and moral lives of the catechists living in the Christian community is integral to the passing on of the faith through their ability to speak from insight into the meaning of divine revelation for the lives of their hearers at the level of catechesis.

The Saints

The great saints, like Augustine and Thomas Aquinas, have always been the most effective communicators of doctrine because they totally incorporated what they believed and professed into a stable way of life. Martyrs do not die for religious propositions. When St. Peter Martyr wrote "Credo" in his own blood when he was killed for opposing heretics, he was not affirming his belief in an ancient deposit of static truth. He proclaimed with his last strength his own vivid awareness of God's constant presence and action in his life.

Pope John Paul II wrote a Holy Thursday Letter to priests in 1986, holding up as a model for them St. John Mary Vianney, a humble parish priest who ministered for some forty-one years in the small town of Ars, France. In spite of the fact that St. John Vianney was almost not ordained because of his inability to master his theological studies, his parish was a flourishing center of faith and a place of pilgrimage for people from all over France and beyond. In 1858, one year before his death, 80,000 pilgrims came to Ars to see and to be ministered to by its saintly pastor.

What was his secret? Not his learning, education, or professionalism. It was his holiness. Pope John Paul II wrote that people came to Ars with the

"realization of meeting a saint, amazing for his penance, so close to God in prayer, remarkable for his peace and humility in the midst of popular acclaim, and above all, so intuitive in responding to the inner dispositions of souls, and freeing them from their burdens, especially in the confessional."[7]

Our respect for science has trained us to look with scepticism on the "miraculous," in our own lives or the lives of others. Yet, in an age similar in many ways to our own, so given to rational enlightenment, what is most noteworthy is that St. John Vianney's pentitents and pilgrims mostly came from the educated rather than the peasant class. Those who sought him out were the ones we would most expect to disregard him. He ministered effectively to magistrates, lawyers, and even officials in the postrevolution anticlerical government of France.

They came in such numbers because St. John Vianney was known to be a saint and, therefore, a powerful channel of divine grace. He was able to articulate for people God's will for them personally, and in so doing, he put them in touch with God. The miracles he worked, and there can be no doubt he worked miracles, deepened the relationship with God of those who sought him out. In fact, his greatest miracles were his insights into the souls of those who came to him for ministering.

Can such a person, so surrounded by legends, so focused on the necessity of a personal relationship to

God in the depths of the human person be a model for preachers, especially catechetical preachers today? Does a preacher who is renowned, not for his theological knowledge and pastoral expertise, but for his austerity, penances, fasting and endless—exhausting— work of service have something to say to preachers today who are far removed from the culture of rural France of the nineteenth century?

The answer is clearly, "Yes." God gives us his saints for all times and places. Sin, repentance, confession, forgiveness are not popular concepts today. They will become popular, however, when catechetists reflect in their preaching the happiness that such gospel values have brought them in their own lives.

Parents

Parents are the first preachers of faith.

"They are the first to communicate the faith to their children and to educate them; by word and example they train their offspring for the Christian and apostolic life" (*Decree on the Apostolate of the Laity*, No. 11).

Indeed, as the "mystery of Christ and his Church,"[8] the family is the primary means God has chosen to establish, maintain, and nourish his people of faith. While the begetting of another human being makes a couple procreators with God himself, to communicate the faith gives them even greater dignity because it makes them procreators of the adopted children of God who will inherit the Kingdom of Heaven.[9]

Raising the adopted children of God far exceeds what mere professionalism can accomplish and demands that catechetical programs be geared in an explicit way to helping parents properly to fulfill their awesome task of forming their children in the faith. Number 78 of the *General Catechetical Directory*, issued by the Sacred Congregation for the Clergy in 1971, specifically enjoins catechetical programs to provide for the adequate formation of parents for their office by competent educators.

Through personal witness, catechetical preaching establishes far-reaching personal relationships with God and one's fellow human beings. Preaching does not just tell us about the historical; it enables us to become Christ. Paul describes what happens to those who hear the gospel message:

"All of us, gazing with unveiled face on the glory of the Lord, are being transformed into the same image from glory to glory, as from the Lord who is the Spirit. . . . For God who said, 'Let light shine out of darkness,' has shone in our hearts to bring to light the knowledge of the glory of God on the face of Jesus Christ" (2 Cor 3:18; 4:6).

Without personal relationships, there would be only ideas, and ideas did not save the world—only Jesus Christ saves the world.

To sum up, two things are required of catechists: the first is that they think intelligently about religion and religious truths. Catechists must know their faith and be able to articulate it in a way that meets the needs of their listeners whatever their age, social background, or educational level. Then catechists must embody their religious reflections in their preaching to make it credible to their hearers.

To revitalize parish catechetical preaching, catechists should be drawn from the elders of the parish, the wisdom people who incarnate in their own persons the revelation of God to their community. While the great theologians with their depth of insight and persuasive argumentation may be able to make the teaching of revelation relevant to the modern world so that their writings awaken a hunger for truth, catechists

make the revelation of God relevant and credible by
their own lived experience of it.

The Example of the Apostle Paul
Paul writes persuasively of the value of suffering as
filling up what is lacking in the sufferings of Christ,[10]
but ultimately he appealed to his own sufferings in
union with Christ to validate his claim to being an authentic teacher as opposed to the "counterfeit apostles" and "dishonest workmen disguised as apostles of
Christ."[11]

We all know instinctively that there is something un-
real about someone who holds up an ideal but fails to
live by it. Even children, or perhaps especially children, can perceive hypocrisy or fraud. Catechists
whose lives do not reflect the joy of the gospel and
who do not live according to the values they proclaim
cannot be effective preachers of the word of God, no
matter how well organized their programs may be.

BIBLE SHARING: AN EFFECTIVE MEANS OF
CATECHESIS
There are many excellent resources available to catechists today that provide information about both teaching methodologies and program content. The field is
so wide, a single book cannot list all the possibilities
for catechesis. However, in the light of the goals and
elements we have ascribed to catechetical preaching,
there is one resource that needs to be used more fully
and directly: the Holy Bible itself.[12]

As we have seen, *The Dogmatic Constitution of Divine
Revelation*, Number 25, stresses the importance of the
Christian people's being intimately familiar with the
word of God from a frequent reading of it. One effective way of familiarizing the faithful with the Bible as
a source of growth in the mystery of Christ is "Bible
sharing."

In this process, small groups of ten to fourteen Christians meet once a week for about one and a half hours to explore the meaning of Scripture together. There are two phases to the exploratory process: first, there is a preparation phase during which the individual members of the sharing group prepare for their weekly meeting by a private, prayerful study of the biblical passages to be shared. In this preparatory phase, they use good Catholic biblical research materials that give the exegetical background of the passage so that the group can interpret it within the orthodox Catholic tradition.

Second, after the completion of the private study, reflection, and prayer, the insights that have been gained from it are shared with the group in the meeting. There are two levels of meaning operative in Bible sharing: (1) the group must understand and appreciate the meaning of the passage arrived at through exegetical study, and (2) it must relate that original meaning of the passage to its significance for Christian life today.[13]

Bible sharing is growing in popularity among Catholics because it is quickly mastered by adult groups. Moreover, it has proven to be extremely popular with young people who are searching for meaning and enjoy the challenge of the quest. Bible sharing puts them into touch with the word of God directly and prepares them to undertake subsequent theological explorations of Catholic tradition in the sacramental programs of catechesis. As a result of Bible sharing's growing popularity, many excellent Bible materials are now being made available for groups to use.

Since Bible sharing needs to be a key part of an integrated faith development program for the whole parish, pastors should motivate all their parishioners to take part in Bible sharing, but there is a special value in it for parish catechists and their students, or perhaps a better term—given the formative character of catechesis—their disciples.

TESTING THE EFFECTIVENESS OF CATECHESIS

How do catechetical preachers know when their catechesis has been effective? In one sense, of course, they can never really know because they are only channels of God's mysterious actions of grace. Preaching communicates on such a profound level of human existence that preachers cannot really identify that particular moment or series of moments when the word of God may bear fruit in the heart and mind of the hearers. Even the listeners themselves cannot always recognize significant moments of growth.

At the same time, there is one sign that indicates whether or not the listeners have grown in their understanding of the word of God and their appreciation of the mystery of Christ in which they are active participants. The beneficiaries of catechesis seek to share the faith in which they have been nourished with others. That is, effective catechesis leads to evangelization by those who have been catechized. If there is no motivation to evangelize, the catechesis has been incomplete. It has, perhaps, succeeded in nourishing a private faith but not the fullness of faith to which the Lord is calling us: "Go into the whole world and proclaim the gospel to every creature" (Mk 16:16).

Pope John Paul II has given catechists a goal to strive for in their preaching ministry when he spoke of the goal of the catechetical ministry in a Catholic university:

"[It] must train young men and women of outstanding knowledge who, having made a personal synthesis between faith and culture, will be both capable and willing to assume tasks in the service of the community and of society in general, and to bear witness to their faith before the world" (*Address to Presidents of Catholic Colleges and Universities*, op. cit.).

With greater particularity, he noted that catechesis also motivates parents to pass on the faith to their children:

"If catechesis is done well, Christians will be eager to bear witness to their faith, to hand it on to their children, to make it known to others, and to serve the human community in every way" (*On Catechesis Today*, No. 24).

NOTES

1. *Apostolic Exhortation on Catechesis in Our Time* (Boston: St. Paul Editions), Number 5.

2. Cf. Romans 10:17.

3. Terence J. Keegan, O.P., *Interpreting the Bible: A Popular Introduction to Biblical Hermeneutics* (New York: Paulist Press, 1985), p. 129. This is an excellent introduction into three recent movements in biblical exegesis that stress the influence of the reader in the process of coming to the meaning of the Bible: structuralism, reader-response criticism, and canonical criticism.

4. Jerry Falwell, "Future-Word: An Agenda for the Eighties" in *The Fundamentalist Phenomenon*, ed. by Ed Dobson and Ed Henson (Garden City: Doubleday and Company, Inc., 1981), p. 220.

5. John Paul II, *Dives in Misericordia* (Hales Corners, WI: Priests of the Sacred Heart).

6. *Address to Presidents of Catholic Colleges and Universities* (op. cit.).

7. "Holy Thursday Letter to Priests." Origins, Vol 15: No. 42, 685–691 (Washington, DC: NC Documentary Service).

8. See Ephesians 5:21–32.

9. See Galatians 4:6,7.

10. Colossians 1:24.

11. Cf. 2 Corinthians 11:12–12:10.

12. *New Catholic World*, Vol 230, No. 1375 (January/February, 1987). The issue is devoted to "The Bible Explosion in the American Catholic Church." In it, major biblical scholars explore the relationship of the Bible to the catechetical, liturgical, and devotional life of contemporary Catholics.

Editor Lawrence Boadt, C.S.P., explains the importance of the explosion:

"There is a major challenge before us to think out how biblical homilies really serve the catechesis of the Church, how worship and liturgy should be coordinated with a deep ongoing devotion to reading the Bible each day, and how creedal and liturgical symbols express biblical proclamations. . . . We cannot wait too long before we give priority to biblical teaching goals and methods. The opportunity is before us now to discover the vitality of a biblically-rooted Catholicism, and we need to grasp it confidently and joyfully."

13. *Bible Sharing: How to Grow in the Mystery of Christ* (New York: Alba House, 1978) describes the process in detail and the *Beginners' Guide to Bible Sharing* (Dubuque, IA: William C. Brown, Co., 1984) provides specific guidelines for discussing and sharing the Acts of the Apostles, the Gospel of Luke, and the Letter to the Romans. Both are by John Burke, O.P.

Chapter Eight

Didascalia

As previous chapters have explained, Christian life comes to the believer through the preaching of the word of God. Evangelization is the first phase of that preaching and begins the life of faith. Catechesis expands that initial proclamation and deepens the faith of the new believer. It gives him the understanding, desire, and power to live in the kingdom of God that is being established on earth through the ministry of the Church of Christ. As the highest form of preaching, didascalia perfects and completes the creative activity of both evangelization and catechesis.

Didascalia is the oral communication of the word of God that brings the Christian who is already an active member of the believing community into the most intimate union with God. In order to do this, didascalia proclaims God's Transcendence and his Immanence.

TRANSCENDENCE

Didascalia reveals God's transcendence; it stresses God's complete otherness from his creatures, in particular, his otherness from human beings. The Psalmist describes the great distance between God and us when he addresses the Lord in prayer:

"Before the mountains were begotten
  and the earth and the world were
    brought forth,
  from everlasting to everlasting you
    are God.

You turn man back to dust,
  saying, 'Return, O children of men.'
For a thousand years in your sight
  are as yesterday, now that it is past,
  or as a watch of the night" (Ps 90:2–4).

This preaching of the divine transcendence puts our human probings into the meaning of life into a healthy, healing perspective. Many of the crises people, even believers, experience today in facing up to and dealing with the reverses of life arise from their lack of appreciation of God's transcendence, omnipotence, and majesty. To be truly satisfying, our relationship to God has to rest on our joyful awareness and grateful acknowledgment that he is sovereignly free. He is under no compulsion to tell us anything about himself. He does not have to communicate with us. God is not answerable to us. In short, God is God and not man. Paul affirms God's transcendence bluntly in his Letter to the Romans:

"But who indeed are you, a human being, to talk back to God? Will what is made say to its maker, 'Why have you created me so?' " (Rom 9:20).

Yet, human beings do have questions about God's ways with us, and frequently they put them to God (or to those whom they perceive as God's representatives) much like journalists question public figures on television. They demand an accounting, and when the answers they are given do not measure up to their standards of acceptability, they deny God's very existence, thus cutting themselves off from any further consideration of ultimate Truth.

For example, many ask: If God is so good, how can he permit so much evil in the world? Why does he not put a stop to the death of innocent children or the sufferings that so often attend the dying? If God exists, why does he let the poor starve, or floods and droughts destroy thousands of human lives?

Underlying this kind of accusatory questioning is the implicit assumption that God must account to us when tragedies occur. This attitude does not comprehend the transcendence of God, and so the human tragedies we all inevitably experience cause severe frustration, confusion, and even despair. Jesus' death on the cross reveals to us Christians, on the other hand, that by submitting to our Father's transcendent glory, we enter into a union of everlasting joy and peace with him.

The Book of Job is the story of one man's struggle to understand the meaning of life. Job's severe sufferings made him question at great length the divine purpose. He recognized that although there seemed to be purpose in the universe, he could not figure out what it was, and so he asked, "Why? Why suffering? Why pain? Why testing?" The Book of Job is very unsatisfying for those who do not value God's transcendence, because, being transcendent, God never did answer Job's questions. At the end of the book, Job comes to realize that while there is order and purpose in God's universe, they exceed the grasp of man's mind. Rather, God's actions flow from a transcendent wisdom that Job was incapable of comprehending. In the end, he could only stand in awe before the divine majesty and accept his sufferings no matter how painful and absurd they seemed to be. For Job, God was, after all, God. And so, the book concludes with Job's humble acknowledgment of the grand design in the things God has made and repentance for having dared to question it:

"I know that you can do all things,
    and that no purpose of yours can be hindered.

I have dealt with great things that I do not
      understand;
   things too wonderful for me, which I cannot know.
I had heard of you by word of mouth,
   but now my eye has seen you.
Therefore I disown what I have said,
   and repent in dust and ashes" (Jb 42:2–6).

IMMANENCE

On the other hand, there are people who acknowledge God's existence but deny the possibility of mean-
ingful relations with him because they conceive of him
only as totally Other. They affirm his transcendence
and power; he created the universe and set things in
motion, but now, they believe, he remains totally
apart. He is unconcerned with individual human lives
today; he does not "interfere" with human activities.
For people who think this way, God does not communicate with us, and we cannot communicate with God.
As the disinterested Beginner of things, the eventual
outcome of our lives and actions is a matter of indifference to him. Such persons lack any appreciation of
God's immanence: his active presence in the universe
and his ongoing concern for and communication with
us his creatures. While theoretically acknowledging
that God exists, they act as if he did not.

TRANSCENDENCE AND IMMANENCE IN JESUS

When the difficulties and sufferings we undergo in life
obscure either God's immanence or transcendence,
true union with God becomes difficult, if not impossible. Hence, didascalic preaching concentrates on developing an appreciation of both God's powerful glory
and his deep love for those fragile beings that he created in his own image and likeness. Didascalia continues the work that evangelization began and catechesis
brought to maturity. Addressing those Christians who
believe in God and who are living in accord with his

179

basic moral demands, this highest form of preaching the word of God reveals how profound a union God seeks with human beings, the glory of all his creation. Jesus expressed the depth of his union by describing it as a permanent dwelling of the Father and himself with his disciples. Jesus said to all those who believe in him:

"In a little while the world will no longer see me, but you will see me, because I live and you will live. On that day you will realize that I am in my Father and you are in me and I in you. . . . Whoever loves me will keep my word, and my Father will love him, and we will come to him and make our dwelling with him" (Jn 14:19,20,23).

DEGREES OF UNION WITH GOD

There are different degrees of union that we can attain with God. At the most basic level, all human beings, Christian or not, can enter into union with God through the things of this world that God created. Since nature is an artifact that is expressive of the divine nature, by studying nature human beings can come to a knowledge, albeit imperfect, of the Creator of nature—the transcendent God:

"Ever since the creation of the world, his [God's] invisible attributes of eternal power and divinity have been able to be understood and perceived in what he has made" (Rom 1:20).

At this most basic level of union, all who are in harmony with nature, delighted by its beauty, awed by its power, and living by its laws are also in harmony with God and his wisdom. In creating the world, God revealed something of himself—his power, his goodness, and his love. Those who live in harmony with nature, therefore, at least implicitly accept the revelation that comes from nature itself and are united to its

Author. In Romans 2:12–16, Paul explains that this union with God through nature alone is also achievable in the moral order. Still, natural union with God is imperfect, and many mysteries in nature and many mysteries in God's design remain to confound the human mind and crush the human heart.

Faith in Jesus Christ raises Christians to a higher degree of union with God. With faith they have a gift that leads them far beyond Job's search for meaning. Christians have the revelation of Jesus, and Jesus answers all the questions of Job, and more, by revealing the ultimate meaning of creation. The universe exists for Jesus; he is the fulfillment of the divine plan that gave birth to creation. Everything that has been created, therefore, finds meaning only insofar as it is united to Jesus. The Letter to the Hebrews tells how God speaks to us through Jesus, for whom he made the universe.

"In these last days, he [God] spoke to us through a son, whom he made heir of all things and through whom he created the universe,
    who is the refulgence of his glory,
      the very imprint of his being,
and who sustains all things by his mighty word.
When he had accomplished purification from sins,
he took his seat at the right hand of the Majesty on
    high" (Heb 1:2,3).

The world was created so that Jesus might deliver us from every evil. When he is completely victorious, the world as we know it will end. Time, then, exists so that all human beings might be united to God for ever. Paul teaches:

"Just as in Adam all die, so too in Christ shall all be brought to life, but each one in proper order: Christ the firstfruits; then, at his coming, those who belong to Christ; then comes the end, when he hands over the kingdom to his God and Father, when he has destroyed every sovereignty and every authority and power. For he must reign until he has put all his enemies under his feet. The last enemy to be destroyed is death, for 'he subjected everything under his feet.' But when it says that everything has been subjected, it is clear that it excluded the one who subjected everything to him. When everything is subjected to him, then the Son himself will also be subjected to the one who subjected everything to him, so that God may be all in all" (1 Cor 15:22–28).

Didascalia is the preaching of divine wisdom. But, since the gift of divine wisdom always leads to the actual living out of what is known and does not stop with merely knowing, didascalia gives Christians the power to live in a complex and troubled world in a way that will bring them into fullest union with God the Father through Jesus Christ in the Holy Spirit. To appreciate the seriousness of the need for didascalic preaching, we explore in some detail how our social activities and our interpersonal relationships lead to our consequent union with God in a conscious and faith-motivated way. Specifically, this chapter will show how the Church's preaching of social justice is a key element of didascalic preaching.

WORKING FOR THE GOOD OF THE HUMAN RACE

We begin this exploration of didascalic preaching by turning to *The Pastoral Constitution on the Church in the Modern World* (*Gaudium et Spes*) of the Second Vatican Council. This document saw the ministry of the Church today as concerned with shaping a better world as well as achieving eternal happiness. The Council wanted:

"to help men gain a sharper insight into their full destiny, so that they can fashion the world more to man's surpassing dignity, search for a brotherhood which is universal and more deeply rooted, and meet the urgencies of our age with a gallant and unified effort born of love" (*Gaudium et Spes*, No. 91).

In that context, *Gaudium et Spes* teaches that we cannot be united to God apart from our union with one another:

"The norm of human activity is this: that in accord with the divine plan and will, it should harmonize with the genuine good of the human race, and allow men as individuals and as members of society to pursue their total vocation and fulfill it" (Ibid., No. 35).

Doing good for the human race obviously benefits the recipients of the Christian's benefactions, while at the same time the Christian himself is also perfected by his service to others:

"Whoever in obedience to Christ seeks first the kingdom of God will as a consequence receive a stronger and purer love for helping all his brothers and for perfecting the work of justice under the inspiration of charity" (Ibid., No. 72).

The point is that the service of our fellow human beings is a particular object of didascalic preaching because such service promotes the fullest union with the Father:

"Mindful of the Lord's saying: 'By this will all men know that you are my disciples, if you have love for one another' (Jn 13:35), Christians cannot yearn for anything more ardently than to serve the men of the modern world ever more generously and effectively. Therefore, holding faithfully to the gospel and benefiting from its resources, and united with every man who loves and practices justice, Christians have shouldered a gigantic task demanding fulfillment in this world. Concerning this task they must give a reckoning to Him who will judge every man on the last day.

"Not everyone who cries, 'Lord, Lord,' will enter into the kingdom of heaven, but those who do the Father's will and take a strong grip on the work at hand. Now, the Father wills that in all men we recognize Christ our brother and love Him effectively in word and in deed. By thus giving witness to the truth, we will share with others the mystery of the heavenly Father's love. As a consequence, men throughout the world will be aroused to a lively hope—the gift of the Holy Spirit—that they will finally be caught up in peace and utter happiness in that fatherland radiant with the splendor of the Lord" (Ibid., No. 93).

The great encyclical letter of Leo XIII, *On the Condition of Labor* (*Rerum Novarum*), which inaugurated the modern Catholic concern for social justice, shows that mankind cannot really achieve justice and live in peace and harmony without recognizing that the purpose of creation goes beyond the finite boundaries of the present world:

"The things of this earth cannot be understood or valued rightly without taking into consideration the life to come, the life that will last forever. Exclude the idea of futurity, and the very notion of what is good and right would perish; nay, the whole system of the universe would become a dark and unfathomable mystery. The great truth which we learn from nature herself is also the grand Christian dogma on which religion rests as on its base—that when we have done with this present life then we shall really begin to live. God has not created us for the perishable and transitory things of earth, but for things heavenly and everlasting; He has given us this world as a place of exile, and not as our true country. Money and the other things which men call good and desirable—we may have them in abundance or we may want them altogether; as far as eternal happiness is concerned, it is no matter; the only thing that is important is to use them right. Jesus Christ, when He redeemed us with plentiful redemption, took not away the pains and sorrows which in such large proportion make up the texture of our mortal life; He transformed them into motives of virtue and occasions of merit; and no man can hope for eternal reward unless he follow in the blood-stained footprints of his Savior. 'If we suffer with Him, we shall also reign with Him.' His labors and His sufferings accepted by His own free will, have marvelously sweetened all suffering and all labor. And not only by His example, but by His grace and by the hope of everlasting recompense, He has made pain and grief more easy to endure; 'for that which is at present momentary and light of our tribulation, worked for us above measure exceedingly an eternal weight of glory' " (*Rerum Novarum*, No. 13).

MYSTICAL UNION WITH CHRIST

Since the Risen Jesus is the fulfillment of God's purpose in creating the universe, a human being can only be in full harmony with nature and God's plan when he lives in union with Christ mystically as well as morally.

"[God] has made known to us the mystery of his will in accord with his favor that he set forth in him as a plan for the fullness of times, to sum up all things in Christ, in heaven and on earth" (Eph 1:9,10).

When we come to the Father by following the teachings of Jesus, we are given freely the answers to the questions over which Job agonized. Jesus reveals to us the meaning of his death as his return to his Father and the ascent into his glory.

"I glorified you on earth by accomplishing the work that you gave me to do. Now glorify me, Father, with you, with the glory that I had with you before the world began" (Jn 17:4,5).

In revealing the meaning of his death, Jesus reveals the meaning of our own death, and all the sufferings that lead up to it. We, through our union with Jesus in death, will join him in glory. Jesus prays for our eternal union with himself at the climactic prayer in John:

"Father, they are your gift to me. I wish that where I am they also may be with me, that they may see my glory that you gave me, because you loved me before the foundation of the world" (Jn 17:24).

Furthermore, the knowledge we gain from our union with Jesus is not just information that gives us a disinterested viewpoint about human suffering. Rather, that revelation has been given to us by Jesus so that we can unite our own pain to Jesus' pain and find total human fulfillment. Paul is so convinced of this truth by the experience of his own pain that he seeks of Christ only

"to know him and the power of his resurrection and [the] sharing of his sufferings by being conformed to his death, if somehow I may attain the resurrection from the dead" (Phil 3:10–12).

As strange and perhaps even as bizarre as it may seem to those without faith in Jesus Christ, the purpose of all human life and of the universe itself is found precisely in preparing for death, because through death we will be able to pass to another, better and happier level of existence that will last forever. The Letter to the Colossians urges us:

"If then you were raised with Christ, seek what is above, where Christ is seated at the right hand of God. Think of what is above, not of what is on earth. For you have died, and your life is hidden with Christ in God. When Christ your life appears, then you too will appear with him in glory" (Col 3:1–4).

The incarnation of the Second Person of the Blessed Trinity is the revelation that God has loved us so much that he has entered into an intimate and permanent union with ourselves. He who is transcendent is also immanent in the lives of all, especially those who live by faith. This revelation of God's love for us, however, has major consequences in terms of how we relate to our fellow human beings.

The First Letter of John emphasizes the importance of loving interpersonal relationships:

"The way we came to know love was that he laid down his life for us; so we ought to lay down our lives for our brothers. If someone who has worldly means sees a brother in need and refuses him compassion, how can the love of God remain in him? Children, let us love not in word or speech but in deed and truth" (1 Jn 3:16–18).

Mystical Love
Didascalic preaching seeks to move the listeners who are already united to God into intimate and full union with him. There are two mutually dependent and inseparable movements of love involved in achieving this union: a movement of love toward God and a movement of love toward fellow human beings. Our love of God is expressed and embodied (though not exhausted) by our love for our fellow human beings. Both movements are the fruit of God's love for us and depend upon his grace.

We are calling this "mystical love" because of the intensity of union with God that it brings about. The term "mystical" has had a variety of meanings attached to it, but perhaps Bergson puts it must succinctly when he says:

"The great mystic is to be conceived as an individual being, capable of transcending the limitations imposed on the species by its material nature, thus *continuing and extending the divine action*" [italics ours].[1]

Through the love that didascalic preaching seeks to foster, the Christian is brought into such intense union with the Father that renewed sources of divine energy are unleashed within him and the listener is able to extend the divine action he experiences within himself into new activities on behalf of the kingdom of God.

In the practical order, therefore, full union with God will lead to full union with our fellow human beings in acts of wholehearted love that may at times call for even heroic self-sacrifice. This two-dimensional love of the supernatural order, the Spirit of God, is the internal principle "which exists effectively in the whole and each of its parts" and that differentiates the "mystical" body of Christ (as Pius XII terms it) from a mere moral union.[2]

The lives of all the great saints, but in a special way, the mystics, attest to this spiritual reality that is the fulfillment of the Law revealed in both New and Old Testaments. When asked which was the greatest commandment in the Law, Jesus replied:

"You shall love the Lord, your God, with all your heart, with all your soul, and with all your mind. This is the greatest and the first commandment. The second is like it: You shall love your neighbor as yourself. The whole law and the prophets depend on these two commandments" (Mt 22:37–40).

Unitive love is at the core of the Church's activity in the world today. Mystical love enables the Christian to have an experience of God that is closer to vision and touch than logical understanding. So Pope John Paul II insists that in order for the Church to fulfill its mission, it must continually reveal the love that is in the Father.

"The reason for her [the Church's] existence is, in fact, to reveal God, the Father who allows us to 'see' him in Christ. No matter how strong the resistance of human history may be, no matter how marked the diversity of contemporary civilization, no matter how great the denial of God in the human world, so much the greater must be the church's closeness to that mystery which, hidden for centuries in God, was then truly shared with man, in time, through Christ."[3]

Inner Harmony
Union with God results in an inner harmony that enables the Christian to effect harmonious relations with his fellow human beings through love. When we speak of harmony, we mean the agreeable and pleasing arrangement of parts, the consistent concordance of elements, a mutual balancing of components into an orderly whole. Hence, for the Christian to be in full union with God, all the elements of his life over which he has control must complement each other for the total good of the Body of Christ. Perfect harmony, of course, can only be achieved in heaven, but heavenly harmony begins on earth, and it has its roots deep within the heart of the individual person. Unfortunately, on earth we often can get an imperfect notion of heavenly harmony only by analyzing the causes of the discord we are experiencing.

St. Paul in the Letter to the Romans describes the destructive disharmony that results when we are unable to control the strong conflicting desires that arise within ourselves. He says:

"What I do, I do not understand. For I do not do what I want, but I do what I hate" (Rom 7:15).

This passage concludes with the agonized cry:

"Miserable one that I am! Who will deliver me from this mortal body?" (Rom 7:24).

When there are unresolved warring factions within the individual, the conflict inevitably spills over into both alienation from God and controversy with others. The Letter of James specifies the social consequences of inner personal turmoil:

"Where do the wars and where do the conflicts among you come from? Is it not from your passions that make war within your members? You covet but do not possess. You kill and envy but you cannot obtain; you fight and wage war. You do not possess because you do not ask" (Jas 4:1,2).

Harmony with God
This same letter of James, which so vividly describes the source of contention and strife between human beings, concludes by attributing the strife between persons (and we might add of nations) to the failure to pray:

"You ask but do not receive, because you ask wrongly, to spend it on your passions" (Jas 4:3).

In other words, the welfare of society is intimately dependent upon the relationship of human individuals to God as suppliants and dependent creatures. Whenever that relationship is violated, the result is social disaster. Unbridled human pride, arrogance, and greed goad people into committing injustices both great and small against others and, in so doing, invoke the wrath of God. The psalmist says:

"Why do you glory in evil,
    you champion of infamy?
All the day you plot harm;
    your tongue is like a sharpened
        razor, you practiced deceiver!

You love evil rather than good,
  falsehood rather than honest speech.
You love all that means ruin,
  you of the deceitful tongue!
God himself shall demolish you;
  forever he shall break you;
He shall pluck you from your tent,
  and uproot you from the land of the living"
  (Ps 52:1–7).

It is easy enough to see the destructive consequences
the psalmist refers to in the godless actions of the nations today. Proud and disdainful rulers tyrannize
their helpless people by denying them their basic human rights. Proud nations expand their borders and
markets at the expense of their neighbors. Leaders pro-
voke war to achieve honor, and their aggression provokes violence in return, which leads thousands upon
thousands of their nations' finest youth to early death.
The rich nations, reveling in their prosperity, subject
the poorer ones to economic enslavement as vassal
states. The pride of race decrees the genocide of "infe-
rior" peoples. All these things are happening in our
own days as much as they happened in ancient times.

THE TEACHING OF SCRIPTURE
The intimate connection between love of God and the
social relationships among individuals and nations is a
major thrust of the teaching of the great prophets of
the Old Testament. Their social teachings, although
coming out of a particular historical context, have validity and applicability for our own times as well.

The prophets warned God's chosen people that because they refused to live according to the Law that
God had given them, they would suffer military de-
feats that would destroy their nation. The fabric of
both their national life and international relations was
inextricably linked to their relationship with God. Two

191

prophets explained why Israel would fall; a third, why a remnant would rise again.

Amos
The prophet Amos was active during a time when Israel was experiencing great material wealth and political power under the kingship of Jeroboam II (783–743 B.C.). It was a glorious time for an Israelite to be alive. However, Amos saw, with prophetic clarity, that Israel contained within itself the cause of the destruction that would soon come upon it. He gave the reasons for Israel's defeat at the hands of the Assyrians:

"Thus says the LORD:
  For three crimes of Israel, and for four,
    I will not revoke my word;
  Because they sell the just man for silver,
    and the poor man for a pair of sandals.
  They trample the heads of the weak
    into the dust of the earth,
    and force the lowly out of the way.
  Son and father go to the same prostitute,
    profaning my holy name.
  Upon garments taken in pledge
    they recline beside any altar;
  And the wine of those who have been fined
    they drink in the house of their god" (Am 2:6–8).

Hosea
Hosea, prophesying shortly after Amos in the eighth century, accurately predicted the fall of the Northern Kingdom to the Assyrians in 721 B.C. He saw the Assyrian victory, which utterly destroyed the Northern Kingdom forever, as the consequence of and divine punishment for the Kingdom's sins against social justice. He said:

"Hear the word of the LORD, O people of Israel,
  for the LORD has a grievance

192

against the inhabitants of the land;
There is no fidelity, no mercy,
  no knowledge of God in the land.
False swearing, lying, murder, stealing and adultery!
  in their lawlessness, bloodshed follows bloodshed.
Therefore the land mourns,
  and everything that dwells in it languishes:
The beasts of the field,
  the birds of the air,
  and even the fish of the sea perish" (Hos 4:1–3).

In a subsequent passage, Hosea attributes the fall of
Samaria to the people's failure to turn to God for political salvation and instead to trust in a political alliance
with Egypt. The fall of the nation, therefore, is the
consequence of the people's relationship to God and
not simply the result of their involvement in international affairs:

"The arrogance of Israel bears witness against him;
  yet they do not return to the LORD, their God,
  nor seek him, for all that
Ephraim is like a dove,
  silly and senseless;
They call upon Egypt,
  they go to Assyria.
Even as they go I will spread my net around them,
  like birds in the air I will bring them down.
  In an instant I will send them captive
    from their land" (Hos 7:10–12).

Zephania
Zephania, a minor prophet of Judah between 640 and
609 B.C., taught clearly that a basic harmony between
the civil life of the Israelites and their relationships
with God would result in an era of peace and material
prosperity for a humble and obedient remnant. Zeph-
aniah said:

"On that day
You need not be ashamed
  of all your deeds,
  your rebellious actions against me;
For then will I remove from your midst
  the proud braggarts,
And you shall no longer exalt yourself
  on my holy mountain.
But I will leave as a remnant in your midst
  a people humble and lowly,
Who shall take refuge in the name of the Lord:
  the remnant of Israel.
They shall do no wrong
  and speak no lies;
Nor shall there be found in their mouths
  a deceitful tongue;
They shall pasture and couch their flocks
  with none to disturb them" (Zep 3:11–13).

The teachings of these three prophets, who are representative of many more whose words are recorded in the Bible, show that personal evil leads to social evil; the faults of the ruler and the faults of his subjects destroy even the most prosperous society. When there is any departure from the norm of justice in the way we deal with one another, we have "sin" and the "punishment" of sin is the intrinsic effect of the injustice itself. Since the effect of injustice is always social, "sin" weakens and eventually destroys the ability of the society to survive. At the same time, when there is harmony in these relationships, the biblical "reconciliation," there is peace.

Prophetic preaching revealed the cause of the social disasters. When prophecy died, the misery of disharmony continued, but the cause of it was hidden. The withdrawal of prophecy was viewed by Amos as the severest of the punishments for sin:

"Yes, days are coming, says the Lord God
   when I will send famine upon the land:
Not a famine of bread, or thirst for water,
   but for hearing the word of the Lord.
Then shall they wander from sea to sea
   and rove from the north to the east
In search of the word of the Lord,
   but they shall not find it" (Am 8:11,12).

Paul

Paul brings the teachings of the prophets to a climactic
moment of revelation when he shows how the failure
to put God into the center of private and social life has
disastrous consequences both for individuals and the
society of which they are a part. Paul says:

"And since they did not see fit to acknowledge God,
God handed them over to their undiscerning mind to
do what is improper. They are filled with every form
of wickedness, evil, greed, and malice; full of envy,
murder, rivalry, treachery, and spite. They are gossips
and scandalmongers, and they hate God. They are in-
solent, haughty, boastful, ingenious in their wickedness, and rebellious toward their parents" (Rom 1:28–
30).

John Paul II

The magisterium of the Church, especially through the
current writings of Pope John Paul II, extends the
scriptural understanding of human behavior as it
seeks to clarify the meaning of "social sins." There is a
rather widespread misconception that there are "institutional" sins that somehow are apart from the personal sins of individuals. In this view, there is an implicit effort to free individuals from responsibility for
the evils that exist in their society. So John Paul II
writes:

"Whenever the Church speaks of *situations* of sin, or when she condemns as *social sins* certain situations or the collective behaviour of certain social groups, big or small, or even of whole nations and blocs of nations, she knows and she proclaims that such cases of *social sin* are the result of the accumulation and concentration of many *personal* sins. It is a case of the very personal sins of those who cause or support evil or who exploit it; of those who are in a position to avoid, eliminate or at least limit certain social evils but who fail to do so out of laziness, fear or the conspiracy of silence, through secret complicity or indifference; of those who take refuge in the supposed impossibility of changing the world, and also of those who sidestep the effort and the sacrifice to avoid, eliminate or at least limit certain social evils but who fail to do so out of laziness, fear or the conspiracy of silence, through secret complicity or indifference; of those who take refuge in the supposed impossibility of changing the world, and also of those who sidestep the effort and the sacrifice required, producing specious reasons of a higher order. The real responsibility, then, lies with individuals"[4]

DIDASCALIA TODAY

This scriptural-magisterial analysis has been necessary in order to put contemporary didascalic preaching into its proper context. So often in the past preaching on fullest union with God has been centered almost exclusively on mystical prayer experiences. The mystic was invited to withdraw from the world, to go apart with Jesus "to a lonely place." His union with God was looked upon as a special holy time, in which the devotee was expected to neglect for awhile his worldly duties and give himself totally to the development of the vertical dimension of his life. It is undeniable, of course, in the light of the long mystical tradition of the Church, that such withdrawal is both desirable and periodically necessary, as, for example, on such occasions as retreats and days of recollection. Nevertheless, Pope John XXIII in his encyclical letter on Christianity and social progress, *Mater et Magistra*, offers a corrective that seems to be required by the contemporary conditions in society:

"We should not foolishly dream up an artificial opposition—where none really exists—between one's own spiritual perfection and one's active contact with the everyday world, as if a man could not perfect himself as a Christian except by putting aside all temporal activity, or as if, whenever he engages in such activity, a man is inevitably led to compromise his personal dignity as a human being and as a believer. Far from this being so, it is perfectly in keeping with the plan of Divine Providence that a man should develop and perfect himself through his daily work. And this work, for almost all human beings, is of a temporal nature."[5]

In other words, a concentration on the individual morality of the past, and the joys of personal union with God through intensive and extensive private devotions, however laudable in themselves, cannot be allowed to distract from the Christian's call to mystical union with God precisely through his efforts to transform society.[6] *The Pastoral Constitution on the Church in the Modern World* (*Gaudium et Spes*) gives a sense of urgency to this modified understanding:

"Profound and rapid changes make it particularly urgent that no one, ignoring the trend of events or drugged by laziness, content himself with a merely individualistic morality. It grows increasingly true that the obligations of justice and love are fulfilled only if each person, contributing to the common good, according to his own abilities and the needs of others, also promotes and assists the public and private institutions dedicated to bettering the conditions of human life" (No. 30).

The *Pastoral Constitution* draws from the entire Judaeo-Christian tradition for its teaching regarding the common good that forms the scriptural and theological basis for didascalic preaching in our time. The *Pastoral Constitution* says:

"God did not create man for life in isolation, but for the formation of social unity. So also 'it has pleased God to make men holy and save them not merely as individuals without mutual bonds, but by making them into a single people, a people who acknowledges Him in truth and serves Him in holiness' (cf. *The Dogmatic Constitution of the Church*). So from the beginning of salvation history He has chosen men not just as individuals but as members of a certain community. Revealing His mind to them, God called these chosen ones 'His people' (Ex 3:7–12), and, furthermore, made a covenant with them on Sinai" (No. 32).

An Eternal Destiny
Although *Gaudium et Spes* does not break new ground in the doctrinal teaching of the Church, it does make one very important contribution to the Church's service of contemporary society. It stresses that God has created us for an eternal destiny, and we cannot fulfill our potential as human beings unless we attain our eternal destiny. This is the heart of the Church's preaching today in these times of such severe crises on so many fronts: crises in the lives of individuals, crises in family life, crises in international relations. So the *Pastoral Constitution* says:

"Faith throws a new light on everything, manifests God's design for man's total vocation, and thus directs the mind to solutions which are fully human.

"This [Second Vatican] Council, first of all, wishes to assess in this light those values which are most highly prized today, and to relate them to their divine source. For insofar as they stem from endowments conferred by God on man, these values are exceedingly good. Yet they are often wrenched from their rightful function by the taint in man's heart, and hence stand in need of purification" (No. 11).

Contemporary "Realism"

The "taint in man's heart" affects many of today's lifestyles. The taint can lead a person to seek practical results without concern for union with God. Expediency replaces morality: if it can be done, do it.

We see immediate applications of this philosophy in modern medicine and economics, to name two important spheres of human activity that wield such enormous influence in today's society. Not every medical procedure science has devised or every business practice the marketplace has developed is thereby moral. They may yield good results in the short term, but all too often, the professional practitioners of these effective methods fail to put the means by which they achieve their goals into the proper context of all human life. *Gaudium et Spes* describes this situation as a contemporary imbalance coming from our modern preoccupation with specialization that results in the personal welfare of individual human beings, and even of larger groupings of society, being sacrificed to the caprice of those who have the ability to manipulate human life to their own advantage.

"Within the individual person there too often develops an imbalance between an intellect which is modern in practical matters, and a theoretical system of thought which can neither master the sum total of its ideas, nor arrange them adequately into a synthesis. Likewise, an imbalance arises between a concern for practicality and efficiency, and the demands of moral conscience; also, very often between the conditions of collective existence and the requisites of personal thought, and even of contemplation. Specialization in any human activity can at length deprive a man of a comprehensive view of reality.

"What results is mutual distrust, enmities, conflicts and hardships. Of such is man at once the cause and the victim" (*Gaudium et Spes*, No. 8).

Obvious examples of this victimization of the innocent are medical procedures that result in abortion or economic policies that benefit employers at the expense of their employees and their families.

Human Solidarity
Didascalic preaching addresses this imbalance by proclaiming our higher destiny that begins to be fulfilled here on earth through the development of human solidarity. There can be a kind of sociological unity apart from our relationship with God, but it is a fragile cohesion that is easily ruptured when the desires of one person or one nation come into conflict with the desires of another. True human solidarity can be maintained only in terms of union with God. *Gaudium et Spes* summarizes the teaching of Scripture regarding God's establishment of a chosen people, first in the Old Testament, then in the New. It concludes by calling everyone to the unity of God's family:

"In His preaching [Jesus] clearly taught the sons of God to treat one another as brothers. In His prayers He pleaded that all His disciples might be 'one.' Indeed, as the Redeemer of all, He offered Himself for all even to the point of death. 'Greater love than this no one has, that one lay down his life for his friends' (Jn 15:13). He commanded His apostles to preach to all peoples the gospel message so that the human race might become the family of God, in which the fullness of the Law would be love. . . .

"This solidarity must be constantly increased until that day on which it will be brought to perfection. Then, saved by grace, men will offer flawless glory to God as a family beloved of God and of Christ their Brother" (*Gaudium et Spes*, No. 32).

SOCIAL JUSTICE FROM MYSTICAL UNION

We cannot enjoy fullest union with God unless we en-. joy loving relationships with our fellow human beings, even to the degree of heroic love. Nor can we carry on effective preaching for social justice apart from deep union with the Trinity. While this is a strong statement, perhaps we are seeing its verification in the lack of any real change in the world situation as a result of preaching today. In fact, the influence of the Church on the modern world seems to be lessening instead of increasing.

In their document, *A Review of the Principal Trends in the Life of the Catholic Church in the United States* (1974), the bishops of the United States observed:

"It is generally recognized that the positive influence of organized religion on public policy and public morality has declined sharply in the United States in recent years."[7]

Regarding members of the Catholic Church in particular, the same document said:

"The pertinent issue now is whether Catholics in the United States are more powerfully formed and influenced by the Church or by secular society. At the very least, many would say that for a large number of Catholics, the influence of secular society—and all that implies, for good as well as ill—counts more heavily than the influence of the Church" (No. 3).

If the evidence from the weakened state of preaching and its lack of effectiveness were not enough, Scripture itself also strongly attests to the need for mystical union with God for effective Christian action, which of course includes life-giving preaching. For example, the Letter to the Hebrews in Chapter 11 vividly describes the heroic strength God gives to those who are united to him through faith.

The Gospels

To live in the truth requires the power of God, as Jesus himself teaches according to the Gospel of John:

"Remain in me, as I remain in you. Just as a branch cannot bear fruit on its own unless it remains on the vine, so neither can you unless you remain in me. I am the vine, you are the branches. Whoever remains in me and I in him will bear much fruit, because without me you can do nothing" (Jn 15:4,5).

We see the need for divine power in the communication of truth clearly exemplified in the Gospel of Matthew, where Jesus' teachings are followed by mighty displays of his power. Chapters 5 through 7 contain the Sermon on the Mount, which summarizes in a succinct form the great teachings of Jesus on the nature of his kingdom and the spirit that animates it. Immediately after "he had come down from the mountain," Matthew recounts a series of ten miracles that show the power of Jesus, and, therefore, testify as to the truth and eternal validity of what Jesus had been teaching. Divine wisdom comes in power.

The Pauline Teaching

Paul explains how the power of God and the teaching of his word sustain the Christian in his efforts to do good to others. This inner resource is especially necessary when we encounter weakness and sinfulness in ourselves and others. Paul wrote:

"For whatever was written previously was written for our instruction, that by endurance and by the encouragement of the scriptures we might have hope. May the God of endurance and encouragement grant you to think in harmony with one another, in keeping with Christ Jesus, that with one accord you may with one voice glorify the God and Father of our Lord Jesus Christ" (Rom 15: 4–6).

The letters of Paul also stress the linkage between human activity and the divine life in man, and Paul's teachings on mystical union are always closely related to concrete directions concerning what is to be done in particular circumstances.

Consider, for example, his teaching regarding the Eucharist. In 1 Corinthians 11:23–34, Paul goes so far as to attribute the deaths and sicknesses the Corinthians are enduring to a punishment from God for their failure to adequately respect the unity of the Christian community. They cause division in the community by the way they eat and drink; they disregard the welfare of the poor; yet, they still have the audacity to celebrate the Eucharist. Paul says that in doing this, they are bringing the wrath of God down upon their heads because "anyone who eats and drinks without discerning the body, eats and drink judgment on himself" (1 Cor 11:29). He concludes by giving specific directions for eucharistic celebration:

"Therefore, my brothers, when you come together to eat, wait for one another. If anyone is hungry, he should eat at home, so that your meetings may not result in judgment. The other matters I shall set in order when I come" (1 Cor 11:33,34).

In 1 Corinthians 12 and 13, Paul teaches that God's gifts, which come to us in a certain hierarchy of values, give us the power to live as we ought, and the way we live is a manifestation, in turn, of God's gifts to us. No matter how valuable the lower gifts are, he says, the exercise of the Christian gift of love that unites us to one another is essential for enduring union with God.

Didascalic preaching, then, unites the mystical and the practical into a single experience of the divine mercy. In the didascalic proclamation of the word of God, the vertical and horizontal dimensions of Christian life become one. The divine and the human blend into a single whole and the corporate and individual aspects of human life are put into a proper relationship. In this way, didascalia brings about our ultimate perfection as members of the Christian community through the fulfilling of our daily responsibilities.

SOCIAL REFORM AND CHRISTIAN PERFECTION
God calls and empowers Christians to transform the world. God requires more of us than merely to live with an anxious anticipation of the end of the world and a hope for deliverance from the catastrophe that will accompany it in the second coming of Christ. God empowers his people to actively engage in the affairs of this world through works of justice and love. Given the nature of preaching as the builder of Christian community, it is clear that the thrust of didascalic preaching is to motivate men and women of faith into even greater action on behalf of the gospel.

At the same time, didascalia does not simply seek social justice, although that is certainly the right of all human beings, believers or not, and, therefore, a goal that Christians should pursue. Activities on behalf of social justice work primarily to effect social reform. They may or may not be addressed to believing Christians; they may or may not be intended to result in faith in Jesus. Didascalia, on the other hand, aims primarily at uniting man with God in immanent communication. This unitive goal of Christian preaching is what distinguishes it from all other forms of communication.

Social Action Burnout

Many who enter enthusiastically into the work of social justice do not persevere in their efforts because they do not operate out of their own mystical union with the eternal Trinity. No one is able to live the Christian gospel in its fullness using only natural resources, and it is impossible to long sustain such a demanding ministry as social justice without the constant influx of divine grace that comes from mystical union.

There is another reason why those engaged in the social ministry may not persevere, even if they are firmly united to Jesus by faith and love: they may have lost sight of the goal of their activity—the building of faith in God and the spreading of his kingdom. Instead, they have gotten trapped into being concerned only about immediate practical concerns and cares. They allow the present necessities of the people they serve to overwhelm them in terms of priorities and energies. Before long, instead of preaching and ministering in a way that leads to union with God, they content themselves to work only for human goals and values, which, although they may be laudable in themselves, are not the stuff by which the world is transformed. Frustrated, then, by repeated lack of results in the projects they have undertaken, they abandon the field to others. To escape this frustration, therefore, it is necessary to bear in mind always God's priorities in all our ministries, including those ministries that aim at promoting the social welfare.

In the first order of priority, God calls all to union with himself and gives his preachers the power to proclaim it. Paul speaks of this as a ministry of reconciliation:

"And all this is from God, who has reconciled us to himself through Christ and given us the ministry of reconciliation, namely, God was reconciling the world to himself in Christ, not counting their trespasses against them, and entrusting to us the message of rec- onciliation. So we are ambassadors for Christ, as if God were appealing through us. We implore you on behalf of Christ, be reconciled to God. For our sake he made him to be sin who did not know sin, so that we might become the righteousness of God in him" (2 Cor 5:18–20).

It takes great faith to sustain Christian social action as an effect of grace and as a means of achieving union with God. Social action needs to be nourished by the hearing of didascalic preaching, the daily reading of the Bible, the wise guidance of the Church, and con- stant prayer.

Rich in Mercy
Pope John Paul II's Encyclical Letter of November 30, 1980, *Rich in Mercy* (*Dives in Misericordia*), is an excel- lent example of the content of didascalic preaching. He begins by stating the principle upon which his let- ter is based:

"Man cannot be manifested in the full dignity of his nature without reference—not only on the level of con- cepts but also in an integrally existential way—to God. Man and man's lofty calling are revealed in Christ through the revelation of the mystery of the Father and his love."[8]

The issue the Pope addresses is that of a contempo- rary understanding of justice that excludes the notion of mercy:

"The present-day mentality, more perhaps than that of people in the past, seems opposed to a God of mercy and in fact tends to exclude from life and to remove from the human heart the very idea of mercy. The word and the concept of 'mercy' seem to cause uneasiness in man, who, thanks to the enormous development of science and technology never before known in history, has become the master of the earth and has subdued and dominated it. This dominion over the earth, sometimes understood in a one-sided and superficial way, seems to leave no room for mercy" (Ibid., No. 2).

The Holy Father then analyzes in great depth the scriptural teaching on the nature of Christian love, of which mercy is an intrinsic element:

"Believing in the crucified Son means 'seeing the Father,' means believing that love is present in the world and that this love is more powerful than any kind of evil in which individuals, humanity or the world are involved. Believing in this love means believing in mercy. For mercy is an indispensable dimension of love; it is, as it were, love's second name and, at the same time, the specific manner in which love is revealed and effected vis-à-vis the reality of the evil that is in the world, affecting and besieging man, insinuating itself even into his heart and capable of causing him to 'perish to Gehenna' " (Ibid., No. 7).

Pope John Paul II concludes his masterful exposition of a central message of the Christian faith by calling upon the Church once again in our own day to proclaim the deepest aspects of the mystery of Christ, which is the work of didascalia. The proclamation of this mystery offers the most practical implications for the happiness of all mankind. He writes:

"The reason for [the Church's] existence is to reveal God, that Father who allows us to 'see' him in Christ. No matter how strong the resistance of human history may be, no matter how marked the diversity of contemporary civilization, no matter how great the denial

of God in the human world, so much the greater must
be the Church's closeness to that mystery which, hidden for centuries in God, was then truly shared with
man, in time, through Jesus Christ" (Ibid., No. 15).

PRESSING ISSUES
The importance of the caution regarding the goal of
didascalic preaching becomes more evident when we
consider certain of the contemporary issues to which
the Church and Christians must address themselves.
There is, for example, the whole area of concern about
nuclear arms. Can this concern in some way be used
as an avenue to union with God? What are the aspects
of the mystery of Christ it reflects? Are there particular
stands on nuclear arms that a good Christian should
take?

Pope John XXIII provided an excellent expression of
the principles for approaching the whole nuclear question when he wrote in *Peace on Earth:*

"Once again we deem it opportune to remind our children of their duty to take an active part in public life,
and to contribute towards the attainment of the common good of the entire human family as well as to
that of their own political community. . . . In other
words, it is necessary that human beings, in the intimacy of their own consciences, should so live and act
in their temporal lives as to create a synthesis between
scientific, technical and professional elements on the
one hand, and spiritual values on the other."[9]

The Challenge of Peace
The Catholic bishops of the United States in addressing the topic of nuclear arms and warfare in their pastoral, *The Challenge of Peace,* recognized that in such a
complex issue there are bound to be differences of interpretation even among Christians of good will. They
wrote:

"When making applications of these [moral] principles we realize—and we wish readers to recognize—that prudential judgments are involved based on specific circumstances which can change or which can be interpreted differently by people of good will (e.g., the treatment of 'no first use'). However, the moral judgments that we make in specific cases, while not binding in conscience, are to be given serious attention and consideration by Catholics as they determine whether their moral judgments are consistent with the Gospel."

To sum it all up, didascalia teaches believing Christians how we can achieve perfect personal, social and religious harmony with the divine purpose and wisdom, and how we can live in intimate union with the omnipotent God who is also our loving Father now and forever.

NOTES

1. Henri Bergson, *The Two Sources of Morality and Reality*, tr. R. Ashley Audra and Cloudesley Brereton with the assistance of W. Horsfall Carter (New York: Henry Holt and Company, 1935), p. 209.

2. Pope Pius XII, *Mystici Corporis*, No. 62.

3. John Paul II, *Dives in Misericordia*, No. 15.

4. John Paul II, *Reconciliatio et Paenitentia* (Vatican City: Libreria Editrice Vaticana), No. 16.

5. Pope John XXIII, *Mater et Magistra* (New York: The American Press, 1961), Nos. 255 and 256.

6. In affirming the importance of social action as an effect of mystical union, we do not mean to deny the validity of the contemplative life. The Second Vatican Council reaffirms its value when it speaks of contemplative communities:

"No matter how urgent may be the needs of the active apostolate, such communities will always have a distinguished part to play in Christ's Mystical body, where 'all members have not the same function' (Rom 12:4). For they offer God a sacrifice of praise, they brighten God's people with the richest splendors of sanctity. By their example they motivate this people; by imparting a hidden, apostolic fruitfulness, they make this people grow. Thus they are the glory of the Church and an overflowing fountain of heavenly graces." (*Perfectae Caritatis*, No. 7). *The Documents of Vatican II*, ed. Walter M. Abbot, S.J., tr. ed. Joseph Gallagher (New York: Guild Press, 1966).

7. *A Review of the Principal Trends in the Life of the Catholic Church in the United States* (Washington, DC: United States Catholic Conference, 1974), No. 2.

8. Pope John Paul II, *Rich in Mercy* (Hales Corners, WI: Priests of the Sacred Heart, 1980), No. 1.

9. Pope John XXIII, *Peace on Earth*, Nos. 146 and 150 in Peter Riga, *Peace on Earth: A Commentary on Pope John's Encyclical* (New York: Herder and Herder, 1963), pp. 242–243.

Chapter Nine

The Eucharistic Homily

The eucharistic homily is a short discourse, the purpose of which is to awaken and deepen in the worshipers a desire to participate fully in the eucharistic liturgy by offering heartfelt praise and thanksgiving to their Heavenly Father through Jesus Christ.

The purpose of the homily is more than just to comment on the meaning of the Scripture passage of the day. In the homily, the preacher manifests to the worshiping community the meaning and power of the eucharistic action, relating the liturgical action to the lives of the worshipers. Through his preaching of the word of God, the homilist shows his listeners how the celebration of the eucharistic sacrifice is a celebration of their own lives of faith. "Homily," therefore, is not so much a word that indicates the content of the discourse at the eucharistic celebration as one that describes the function preaching fulfills in that celebration.

For example, there are different aspects to the eucharistic liturgy: it is praise and thanksgiving (eucharist); it is participation in the body and blood of the Lord—a sharing in the one bread, a drinking of the one cup (communion). It is also sacrifice—the representation of the Sacrifice of Calvary under signs and symbols that were originated by the Lord himself at the Last Supper. Hence, it is a powerful and grace-filled ritual of the community, which is both summit and source of the Christian life.[1]

The homilist properly focuses his preaching on one or other of these aspects, using his proclamation of the word of God to motivate the congregation to participate more fully in the act of worship. He does this by recalling to their minds the gifts that the Lord has given his people throughout history. This memory of past favors, in turn, enables them to recognize God's continuing gifts to them in their own daily lives today. In this way, the eucharistic homilist motivates the people toward an enthusiastic outpouring of praise and thanksgiving for the gifts they have been given.

The word of God that the homilist preaches is, therefore, an integral part of the liturgy. He draws on both Scripture and tradition, which "form one sacred deposit of the word of God,"[2] to reveal the present significance of the liturgical act. By proclaiming the word of God, he rouses his hearers to deeper acts of belief in the presence, power, and love of God, and greater trust in God's saving action in their lives.

When the Christian people are fully aware, in faith, of what they are doing, the effects of the sacraments go far beyond the immediate celebration itself. The liturgy communicates the grace of the Risen Jesus to the worshipers for incarnation in all aspects of their lives. The liturgy not only reflects the people's faith, which it must do, of course; it also nourishes the faith of the celebrating community. It gives them an opportunity for corporate worship, and at the same time it also gives them the power and the desire to worship God outside liturgy in everything they do.

This extension of the celebration keeps the liturgy from becoming a kind of closed entity: a complex ritual act that is merely historically significant and only artistically attractive. The homily relates the reality of sacramental mystery to the reality of the daily life of the people, as individuals and as a community of God's royal priesthood.

Thus, homiletic preaching creates the environment of faith that makes possible the celebration of liturgy. It fuses the liturgical action with the lives of the worshipers. And finally, it deepens the spiritual awareness of the people to Christ's presence among us.

The Importance of the Homily
The liturgical homily is mentioned frequently: in the *Code of Canon Law* (c. 767), in the liturgical books, especially Number 41 of the *Instruction on the Roman Missal*, and in numerous papal decrees and statements issued since Vatican II. It is frequently mentioned because the homily is vitally important to the life of the Church. Hence, homilists are being continually urged to devote time and careful study to the preparation of effective, faith-transmitting homilies.

Because of its importance, the Church carefully legislates when the homily is to be preached, by whom and its basic content.

"The most important form of preaching is the homily, which is part of the liturgy, and is reserved to a priest or deacon. In the course of the liturgical year, the mysteries of faith and the rules of christian living are to be expounded in the homily from the sacred text" (c. 767, 1).

The basic liturgical directive in the *Instruction on the Roman Missal* says that the homily is to be given on all Sundays and feasts of obligation. This is repeated in Canon 767:

"At all Masses on Sundays and holydays of obligation, celebrated with a congregation, there is to be a homily and, except for a grave reason, this may not be omitted.

"It is strongly recommended that, if a sufficient number of people are present, there be a homily at weekday Masses also, especially during Advent and Lent, or on a feast day or an occasion of grief.

"It is the responsibility of the parish priest or the rector of a church to ensure that these provisions are carefully observed."

Homilies are also obligatory at liturgical services apart from the eucharist. Homilies are to be preached at all stages of the Rite of Christian Initiation of Adults (RCIA), at the baptism of infants, and at confirmation. It is also to be preached at communal celebration of reconciliation, weddings, funerals, ordinations, and anointings of the sick.

Like the eucharistic liturgy, each of the other sacramental liturgies celebrates its own unique aspect of Christian dying, rising, and sharing—the paschal mystery as lived out in the lives of the faithful. Hence, the homilies preached at the different sacramental liturgies should be aimed at arousing and nourishing those aspects of faith that are most appropriate to the celebration.

The Church, in her wise liturgical tradition, which stretches over so many centuries, helps its preachers in this essential revelatory and empowering task. It has selected certain Scripture passages that are particularly appropriate to the power of the sacrament being celebrated, and it encourages its preachers to draw on them for their inspiration and insights.

For example, the baptismal homily develops the teaching of Paul for those celebrating the baptismal liturgy:

"We who were baptized into Christ Jesus were baptized into his death. We were indeed buried with him through baptism into death, so that, just as Christ was raised from the dead by the glory of the Father, we too might live in newness of life" (cf. Rom 6:3,4).

By preaching the word of God, the homilist encourages, indeed empowers, the recipients of the saving water to make a deep act of faith in the Lord Jesus as their Savior. While baptism confers the grace of conversion, it is also the liturgical and communal celebration of the initiating grace of Christ that has brought the believers to this moment. Baptism both effects and ratifies faith in Christ. Through baptism the convert gains entry into the believing community.

If the newly baptized has not yet reached the age of discernment so that he is able to make his own personal act of faith, that act of faith is made for him by the Church. The power of the word of God arouses the members of the Church participating in the liturgy to acts of faith on behalf of the child.

Confirmation, the sacrament of Christian maturity, strengthens Christians for witnessing to the Lord; it gives them the power to share their faith with others, thus bearing the fruit called for by the command of Jesus. Therefore, the preaching of the word of God in this celebration both reveals the power being received and motivates the recipients to reach out and share what they have received with others through the powerful outpouring of the Spirit.

The anointing of the sick strengthens Christians to endure and to be strengthened in time of great need, at a critical point in the lives of Christians. The word of God preached at this period of illness manifests to them the presence of Christ and his concern for their well-being that brings about a renewed outpouring of divine life. Since sin weakens us in our efforts to serve God, the sacrament of the anointing first forgives the sins of suffering Christians. By freeing them from their sins, the sacrament communicates the power for them to bear all things for the sake of Christ. When it is God's will, the sacrament also effects a physical and mental healing, so that they are restored to full service in the Lord.

In the sacrament of reconciliation, whether communally celebrated or auricularly (all liturgical acts are, of course, public), the homily creates in the hearts of the penitents trust in the forgiveness they are receiving in the sacrament.

The ritual also calls for homilies when persons are instituted in the ministry of lector and acolyte and admitted to candidacy for sacred orders. The profession ceremonies of religious, the consecrations of virgins, the blessings of abbots and abbesses, the dedications of churches, altars, and the blessings of foundation stones—all these call for the preaching of liturgical homilies.

Furthermore, since the homily is an integral part of the liturgy, ordinarily the celebrant of the liturgy is the homilist. Certain exceptions are allowed, however. Thus, another priest or even a deacon may be permitted to preach in place of the celebrant if the circumstances require it, but this is not to become the usual practice of a parish.

While the liturgical books never refer to a lay person as a homilist, for the reasons we have previously treated in Chapter Two, a lay person can give an additional address in the course of the Mass. In no way, however, should the address be a duplication of or a substitution for the homily preached by the celebrant or ordained minister. Not even the bishop has the authority to dispense from this legislation of the Church.

The Goal of the Liturgical Homily

Given its importance, the liturgical homily is probably also the most difficult and demanding form of preaching there is because it can be addressed to a community celebrating faith that includes those needing evangelization, those needing catechesis, and those hungering for didascalia. The homilist has to relate to these different levels of faith need all at the same time.

Moreover, since the homily deals with the mystery of Christ-among-us being celebrated in the liturgy, it has to convey a sense of the meaningfulness in Christ of human life in this world. As a result, the effective homily, like the Bible, will inevitably stimulate more questions than it answers, but the questioning and the pondering that result will lead to further growth in faith.

The eucharistic homilist cannot achieve this complex goal simply by giving doctrinal instructions or liturgical explanations. Furthermore, the homily demands more from the preacher than simply giving pieces of good advice or exhorting the people to live their lives in accord with the moral law. The nature of the homilist's task, in other words, is more than simply "applying" the biblical texts to contemporary living, which seems to be a widespread understanding of what homiletic preaching is.

The preaching of the word of God in the liturgy leads the worshiping community more deeply into a life of contemplation. From the life of contemplation, in turn, will flow truly Christian behavior and witness. By presenting the rich gospel message, the homilist gives individual Christians the principles by which, under the special movements of the Holy Spirit, they will be able to make their own decisions as to how best to incarnate the word of God in their own lives and to live in accordance with their own vocations. The homilist provides the word of God as nourishment for his listeners' Christian maturity.

Only the individual can really know how he can live in union with the Lord, because only he is fully cognizant of the diverse circumstances that must be taken into account in determining specific action. Ultimately, only the individual is capable of discerning the moments of grace in his life and movements of grace in the depths of his being. Consequently, only the individual can recognize God's call to him and appreciate the interior expectations of service the Lord has placed upon him. Eli, for all his experience and wisdom in the ways of God, could only tell Samuel to go back and wait for the Lord to speak.[3]

The Declaration on the Ministry and Life of Priests (Number 6) instructs priests to respect the individuality of those to whom they preach, and, therefore, its instruction is particularly pertinent to eucharistic homilists:

"As educators in the faith, priests must see to it, either by themselves or through others, that the faithful are led individually in the Holy Spirit to a development of their own vocation as required by the gospel, to a sincere and active charity, and to that freedom with which Christ has made us free. Liturgies, however beautiful, or associations however flourishing, will be of little value if they are not directed toward educating men in the attainment of Christian maturity."

By being sensitive to the complexity of the word of God in relation to the circumstances of daily Christian life, the homilist will be able to lead the people into a greater awareness of God in all they do. He will enable them to see their whole life as a spiritual sacrifice truly pleasing to God. His preaching will help them turn everything they do into an *eucharistia* that responds to the appeal of Paul:

"I urge you therefore, brothers, by the mercies of God, to offer your bodies as a living sacrifice, holy and pleasing to God, your spiritual worship. Do not conform yourself to this age but be transformed by the renewal of your mind, that you may discern what is the will of God, what is good and pleasing and perfect" (Rom 12:1,2).

Alexander Schememann sums up the functional goal of the homily:

"The liturgical homily prevents the liturgy from becoming an end in itself, but makes it an epiphany of the Church's faith, of her experience in Christ, of herself, the world and the Kingdom."[4]

Contemporary Problems
Contrary to this broad understanding, many homilists and their congregations are locked into a rather repetitious pattern of somewhat superficial commentary only on the gospel text of the day. This is causing serious difficulties for spiritual growth in parishes.

For example, if the homilist never preaches on anything except the Sunday gospel texts, the Christian vision of the his parish will be only historical. That is, his parishioners may well become familiar with the gospel stories of God's saving action in the past, but they may not be led to perceive the Risen Savior's present action in their own lives. At the very least, therefore, frequent preaching on the Pauline letters and the other apostolic letters, which are addressed directly to believing Christians of all generations, is necessary to form parishes in the dynamic, Spirit-led aspects of Christian life of which Paul, in particular, was such a great communicator.

Today the Church in the United States is undergoing an extreme reaction to its previous practice of extensive catechetical instruction at Mass. Such catechesis in the past was usually unrelated to the eucharistic celebration. On the other hand, a too-strict interpretation of "homily" as a commentary on the gospel text of the day or a commentary on a Mass theme common to all three Sunday readings has resulted in large numbers of Americans being deprived of continuing nourishment in the basic mysteries of their faith because these mysteries do not find expression in the Scripture pericopes chosen for the Sunday Masses. The consequences of this kind of restricted preaching can be seen in the growing number of failing marriages, the lack of vocations to any kind of dedicated life, low standards of morality, the widespread lack of participation in church activities—sacramental, educational, or social—and the meager efforts at evangelization.

Obviously, more effective preaching of the Sunday homily cannot alone change this truly depressing state of affairs. Nevertheless, a renewal in the preaching of the Sunday homily does have an important contribution to make. Sunday Mass is still a significant part, actually in most cases the major part, of a practicing Catholic's religious life. Sunday Mass participation is the greatest link most practicing Catholics have with the Risen Jesus, and the word of God they hear at Mass is the most significant source of their growth in their knowledge of the mystery of Christ among us.

To nourish that kind of perceptive and experiential faith and hope at Mass, homilists have to draw upon the entire tradition of the Christian Church. Commenting on isolated pericopes in the lectionary is not enough. The pericopes can be connected to one another in the lectionary through the liturgical cycle. It does not follow, however, that the listeners perceive them as connected to one another or, more importantly, to their own lives.

Although the Church has greatly expanded the selection of readings over the course of three years, the lectionary alone cannot possibly provide adequately developed material for the kind of nourishing preaching the liturgy itself calls for and the *Constitution on the Sacred Liturgy* demands. Indeed, the pericopes chosen for the lectionary presume that the faithful are reading the Bible on their own as a continuing, life-long, self-learning growth in the word of God that is then celebrated in the believing community. Such, however, is generally not the case.

What is needed, therefore, is a homilist who is a communicator to the People of God and one who can articulate his own experienced vision of the Christian message as we have been describing it in this book. His vision, under the impetus of the Holy Spirit and the guidance of the Church, rises out of his own struggles of faith, his own understanding of the Scriptures, his own formation in divine wisdom and love, and his own intimate life with Christ in close union with the Church.

The homilist needs to preach out of all his God-given experiences in the gospel. He needs to explore creatively all aspects of the Church's life so he can communicate the full gospel message. He will never be able to do that if he only talks about a specific few verses of Scripture Sunday after Sunday, year after year.

If there is to be a renewal in liturgical preaching, such as that for which the ancient Fathers were renowned, homilists must once again personally search the Scriptures. This search, of course, requires a familiarity with Sacred Scripture, but it also demands continual prayer and an ongoing action of the Holy Spirit.

Fortunately, practical pastoral reform and renewal of the eucharistic homily are possible because of the inspired teaching of the Second Vatican Council. The Conciliar Fathers, well aware of the decline of faith and the intense need for revitalized biblical and liturgical preaching, freed the homily at Mass to become an exciting instrument of the communication of divine truth as lived daily by Christians and celebrated in the sacred rites of our religion, especially in the eucharistic liturgy.

The issue of the reform of liturgical preaching was directly and forcefully addressed by the Fathers of the Second Vatican Council. Nowhere is this call for revitalization more evident than in their formulation of the *Constitution on the Sacred Liturgy*. In this document, the first to be promulgated, the Council made very specific counsels, which when faithfully implemented, will result in the hoped for renewal of the liturgical, especially eucharistic homily. In legislating this reform, the Fathers sought a return to the glorious homiletic tradition of the early Church.

The Roots of Reform[5]
The eucharistic preaching of the early Christian communities was patterned on the preaching in the Jewish synagogues. Synagogue preaching was basically a simple, informal explanation of selected texts of Scripture that sought to connect what God had done in the past to the present needs and circumstances of the community. Jesus' preaching at the beginning of his ministry in Galilee, in Luke 4:16–30, is a good example of this tradition.

After the Resurrection, when the apostles and eyewitnesses of Jesus' ministry began to preach, they continued to use synagogue preaching as the model for their proclamation of the Good News. Paul, for example, preached in the synagogue to the Jews of Pisidian Antioch.[6]

Under the impulse of the Holy Spirit, they found in the sacred texts they used in their primitive liturgies the mysterious and powerful presence of the Risen Lord Himself. The miracles they were able to perform were validation of their preaching, even as Jesus' miracles were the signs of the truth of his preaching.[7]

When these first preachers began to die off, and it became evident that the Second Coming of Christ was not going to occur as soon as had been expected, the Christian community committed the substance of the apostolic preaching to writing in the form of gospels and letters. These writings, in turn, were read in the liturgies and became themselves the basis of commentary and explanation by the early preachers. In these new sacred books, through their preachers, the community came into the presence of Christ himself.

Throughout the first century, the preaching in the community celebrations was done by a variety of persons (evangelists, prophets, teachers, etc.) who were recognized by the community as called by God. Exercising real teaching authority, they commented on particular texts of Sacred Scripture and compared them to other pertinent passages in the Bible. In particular, they related the events of Christ's life to the prophecies of the Old Testament. In so doing, they drew heavily on their own personal experiences of the Spirit of Christ as they sought to communicate with divine authority the relevancy of the biblical text for their own day.

In the early years of the second century, the traveling evangelists and prophets became less influential and preaching began to be restricted to those upon whom the community had laid hands; that is, bishops. Preaching by priests and deacons did not come until much later. These ordained preachers interpreted the

223

Scriptures within the liturgical celebration, leading to the development of a Christian rhetoric. Origen (185–253) gave this preaching the name "homily." From this point on, the homily form develops somewhat differently in the Eastern and Western Churches.

The Homily in the Eastern Church

As used by Origen, homily signified a preaching within the liturgy that sought to relate it to the great historical events of salvation. The preacher spoke to his audience in ordinary and simple language, endeavoring to help them find in revelation the answers to their present difficulties. For Origen, preaching was "a mutual search by preacher and congregation—a seeking after the voice of God."[8]

The eastern Fathers of the second and third centuries continued the evolution of the homiletic form by searching the Scriptures diligently to find there the divine meaning they could communicate to their people. In so doing, they showed that Christ himself is present as the powerful word of God. Their preaching still closely resembled the synagogue practice of informal preaching.

A growing interest in and use of rhetorical devices in the fourth century diminished the informality that had been so characteristic of earlier preaching. Furthermore, instead of commenting on selected texts, the preaching of this century was more apt to develop particular scriptural or theological themes as part of doctrinal instruction. Finally, the Fathers sought to reveal the mystery-presence of Christ in the sacramental celebrations of which they were a part.

The Greek homily reached its apex in the preaching of St. John, Patriarch of Constantinople (350–407). Known as "Chrysostom," i.e., of the Golden Mouth, his preaching is a model of the Greek homily because he expressed with great eloquence the "keen feelings, the living ideas, the earnest practical lessons that he had to communicate to his hearers."[9]

The Homily in the Western Church

Tertullian (160–220) was the first of the great Latin Fathers to give the homily its peculiar Latin character, which put more emphasis on the reality of sin and its consequences in human life than on the glory that comes with faith in Christ.

Over a century later, Augustine (354–430) inaugurated a new way of preaching in the Western Church. Although trained in the finest rhetorical schools, Augustine emphasized the importance of content over the rhetorical form. He preached on how the sacraments manifested the presence of Christ revealed in the Scriptures.

Following Augustine, the informal, but so often eloquent, Greek homily form began to fall into desuetude as preachers in the west used the more formally structured Latin "sermo" or sermon.

Another significant development in the western homily took place during the fifth and sixth centuries. During this period, the liturgy as it was celebrated at the papal court became normative for the entire Western Church. The papal liturgy was elaborate and highly developed, and so led to increased concern for rhetorical form and structure in the liturgical sermon. The sermons of this time, in particular those of Leo the Great (Pope: 440–461), concentrated on developing liturgical themes and moral teaching rather than on exegeting and explaining Scripture. Pope Leo himself is remembered for his commentaries on the feasts celebrated in the evolving liturgical year.

A number of the developments that took place during this period were incorporated centuries later in the

Constitution on the Sacred Liturgy. One that stands out, for example, is the great emphasis on the liturgy's making present the salvific events of Christ's life. Thus, for both Leo and ourselves, Easter is the central saving event that is at the heart of our liturgical celebrations.

Because the liturgy and the sacraments were viewed as celebrating the presence of Christ's saving events among us, the preachers at these liturgies themselves were perceived as having a sacramental value in that they represented in their own person the presence of Christ. Therefore, Leo reaffirmed the custom dating back to the second century and allowed only bishops and priests to preach.

Priests did not begin to preach in great numbers until the Council of Vaison in 529. Until that time, it was usually the bishops who preached. However, the increased number of Christians required that the preaching ministry be shared with priests. This practice was formalized in a decree of the Council of Vaison, "for the edification of all the churches and the benefit of all the people not only in the cities but also in the rural areas."

The same Council also declared:

"If, because of illness, the priest is unable to preach let the homilies of the holy fathers be read by the deacons."[10]

With Gregory the Great (Pope: 590–604), the age of the great Fathers came to an end. While Gregory's excellent handbook on preaching, *The Book of Pastoral Care,* was very influential, nonetheless, in Gregory's time, preaching became less important in the liturgy and took second place to ritual acts, especially in the celebration of the sacraments and the offering of the official prayer of the Church.

Today, when Christianity is again in decline in the western world where it has held sway for so long, the Church once again turns to the preaching of the word of God to revitalize its ministry to the world. Central to this revitalization is a renewed attention to the importance and nature of the eucharistic homily in liturgical legislation.

HOMILETIC LEGISLATION

The Constitution of the Sacred Liturgy

The Second Vatican Council established the homily as the link between the word of God and the Eucharist in its first document, *The Constitution on the Sacred Liturgy*. Article 35, paragraph 2, says:

"Because the sermon is part of the liturgical service, the best place for it is to be indicated even in the rubrics, as far as the nature of the rite will allow; the ministry of preaching is to be fulfilled with exactitude and fidelity. The sermon, moreover, should draw its content mainly from scriptural and liturgical sources, and its character should be that of a proclamation of God's wonderful works in the history of salvation, the mystery of Christ, ever made present and active within us, especially in the celebration of the liturgy."

Making the sermon an integral part of the liturgical celebration marks a significant development in the Church's understanding of its liturgical life. *Mediator Dei*, the encyclical letter of Pope Pius XII on the liturgy, was written in 1947, sixteen years before the Second Vatican Council. At that time, Pope Pius XII assumed the presence of faith in those who took part in the sacramental life of the Church, and his letter was content to exhort the faithful to come to the liturgy with proper dispositions.

"While we stand before the altar, then, it is our duty so to transform our hearts that every trace of sin may be completely blotted out, while whatever promotes supernatural life through Christ, may be zealously fostered and strengthened even to the extent that, in union with the Immaculate Victim, we become a victim acceptable to the Eternal Father" (*Mediator Dei*, No. 100).[11]

The same encyclical viewed the readings, sermons, vestments, and the external splendor of the liturgical rites as an enhancement of the proper dispositions for participation in the liturgy:

"All these things aim at enhancing the majesty of this great Sacrifice, and raising the minds of the faithful by means of these visible signs of religion and piety, to the contemplation of the sublime truths contained in the Sacrifice" (*Mediator Dei*, No. 101).

The Second Vatican Council, however, no longer viewed the sermon as a mere "enhancement" of liturgy or even an interruption[12] of the sacred rite, which could be rather easily omitted and which did not bind the faithful to listen. It became a part of the liturgy itself, and the decrees of the Council and the subsequent legislation of the Church reflect that new understanding.

Article 52 of the *Constitution on the Sacred Liturgy*, while continuing to give eucharistic preaching a firm scriptural foundation, reflects the open-ended approach of the Conciliar Fathers to the eucharistic homily:

"By means of the homily the mysteries of the faith and the guiding principles of the Christian life are expounded from the Sacred Text during the course of the liturgical year."

This article supersedes Canon 1345 of the old Canon Law, which had encouraged the Sunday Mass homily to treat of such subjects as "a brief explanation of the Gospel or some part of Christian doctrine."

Although in agreement regarding the importance of the homily and its scriptural focus, the Conciliar Fathers did not arrive at the final formulation of Article 52 without considerable debate. The article went through five different stages before the present version was accepted. Unfortunately, in spite of extended debate and many revisions, the questions concerning the proper content of the homily were never resolved, and the final formulation of Article 52 reflects the conciliar uncertainty.

In one effort to establish exact guidelines for what constitutes the proper content of the homily. Bishop Charles-Marie Himmer of Tournai, Belgium, wanted to describe the homily as a commentary by the celebrant on the readings proclaimed at Mass.

Others were opposed to such a restricted view of the homily. They wanted the *Constitution* to be unmistakably clear that preaching at Mass should concern itself with all aspects of the Christian faith, drawing upon the range of resources available to the homilist. As a result and for varying specific reasons, a number of bishops suggested that the term "sermon" replace the term "homily," or at least be used in addition to it.

Subsequent interventions in the debate stressed the importance of catechesis. Some bishops called for a syllabus of catechetical instruction to govern what was preached; they urged the teaching of all Christian doctrine over a period of four to five years based on the liturgical texts. Some wanted to use the term "catechesis" in place of "homily" because they perceived that the latter term was open to serious misunderstandings. (Events have proven their fears to be well-founded.) Finally, others wanted the *Constitution* to make explicit that not only were the scriptural roots of Christian teaching to be treated in the homily; preachers were to deal with dogmatic and moral aspects as developed by theologians as well.

Throughout the lengthy debate, and directly as a result of these varied interventions, the Liturgical Commission strove mightily to understand and express more precisely the relationship between the homily, the liturgy, and the total exposition of Christian doctrine. Basically, the Commission saw the homily as an explanation of the readings that were proclaimed at Mass throughout the entire course of the liturgical cycle. Hence, the Commission proposed the *Constitution* mandate a wider selection of Scripture readings in order to make it easier to cover the entire Christian teaching over a period of time.

A crucial point pertinent to our purposes now emerged in the debates both within the Commission and in the Council itself over Article 52. One of the Conciliar Fathers wanted the article to state explicitly that the homily had to be based on a Sacred Text *taken from the Mass of the day*. The Liturgical Commission responded that although "by its nature" the homily should be on the text read in the Mass at which the homily is preached, nevertheless, the Commission said, even some of the Ancient Fathers of the Church were accustomed to compose their homilies on other texts. As a result, the Liturgical Commission opposed the introduction of that stringent restriction into the final version, and the Council agreed with its position because nowhere in the *Constitution* was that limitation ever incorporated.

These extensive debates revealed that the bishops and their advisors were unsettled about what a homily is and what it is supposed to do. The Liturgical Commission showed its own ambivalence by distinguishing between the "nature" of the homily and the practice of the ancient Fathers without anywhere exactly defining what that "nature" is.

The ambivalence of both Commission and Council is further manifest in the difference between Article 52 and Article 35, paragraph 2, of the *Constitution* quoted above. Article 52 describes the homily as an exposition of the mysteries of faith and the guiding principles of Christian life "from the Sacred Text during the course of the liturgical year." Article 35, on the other hand, only requires that the homily "draw its content mainly from scriptural and liturgical sources" without further specification. Indeed, the only specification it makes is that its character should be that of a proclamation of God's works and Christ's presence and activity.

Such vagueness in speaking of the eucharistic homily in the *Constitution* has left the issue open to subsequent interpretations that may or may not reflect the intention of the Council. The core issue remained unresolved: Given the fact that most Catholics have the opportunity to hear the word of God only at Sunday Mass, how can homilies serve to prepare them for eucharistic celebration at which they are present (mystagogical function), and at the same time, teach them in some consistent and progressive way the truths that are necessary for salvation (catechetical function)?

In short, the question of how the homily as a commentary on the Scripture readings can also be invested with a catechetical character was never settled in the *Constitution*.

Subsequent instructions have not been able to do any better in reconciling the two values. Instead, what was explicitly excluded by the Council is being forced into Church praxis by later instructions that lack the inspired authority of Conciliar thought.

Restrictive Interpretations

The earliest instruction on the implementation of the *Constitution on the Sacred Liturgy, Inter oecumenici* (September 26, 1964), No. 54, begins the process of restrictive understanding explicitly rejected by the Council when it states:

"The 'homily from the sacred text (CSL, No. 52)' is to be either an explanation of certain aspects of the readings from the Sacred Scriptures or of some other text from the Ordinary or Proper *of the day* taking into account, however, peculiar needs of the Congregation."

At the same time, even this more restrictive document leaves open the possibility of a catechetical preaching plan. Number 55 of *Inter oecumenici* says:

"If a scheme for preaching is drawn up for certain times of the year, it should be closely and harmoniously linked with at least principal seasons and feasts of the liturgical year (cf. CSL, Arts. 102–104). It should be linked, that is to say, with the mystery of redemption. The homily is part of the liturgy of the day."

A later instruction of the Congregation of Rites, May 25, 1967, *Eucharisticum mysterium*, Article 10, favors the mystagogical function of the homily, not limiting the homily specifically to the gospel pericope or pericopes of the day. It says:

"The purpose of the liturgy of the word [is] to develop the close connection between the preaching and the hearing of the word of God and the eucharistic mystery. . . . In this way, the faithful will be nourished by the word of God which they have received and in a spirit of thanksgiving will be led to a fruitful participation in the mysteries of salvation."

Nevertheless, the struggle between the mystagogical and catechetical tensions of the liturgy goes on. The

Institutio Generalis of the revised *Missale Romanum* of March 26, 1970, reflects the more restrictive understanding of the homily rejected by the Council. Number 41 states:

"The homily is strongly recommended as an integral part of the liturgy and as a necessary source of nourishment for the Christian life. It should develop some point of the readings or of another text from the Ordinary of the Mass *of the day*. The homilist should keep in mind the mystery that is being celebrated and the needs of the particular community."

Consequences of Restriction

This restrictive understanding of the homily causes special difficulties for the Church in America, where there has been a very strong catechetical emphasis in Sunday Mass preaching. Preaching plans, called syllabi, were common diocesan practice. These plans assured that the faithful would receive a progressive formation in the basic truths of the faith over a prescribed period of time. The plans necessarily required the use of source materials outside the Mass's Scripture texts.

Yet, in spite of the strength of that catechetical tradition so frequently reinforced over the years by diocesan synods throughout the country, a survey conducted by Robert F. McNamara for the Word of God Institute in 1975 revealed that the majority of dioceses follow the restrictive interpretations of the *Constitution*, even at the sacrifice of catechetical continuity.

In this regard, Fr. McNamara makes a singularly important observation:

"The peril of the situation is that many contemporary Catholics (I dare not guess how many), during the past decade, must have been told or reminded all too little, from the uniquely important Sunday pulpit, of some basic points of Christian doctrine. Whether this is yet a tragic situation, it is a dangerous one; and I am convinced that it demands prompt study and remedy.[13]

In the light of the seriousness of the present crisis—glaringly revealed in the latest sociological statistics regarding religious practice and morals—we do well to recall constantly that the Council never outlawed catechetical preaching plans. Moreover, *Inter oecumenici*, No. 55, specifically allows periodic preaching plans, as long as the plan is "closely and harmoniously linked with—at least—the principal seasons and feasts of the liturgical year."

Canon 767, 1, in the new code is the last legislation issued on this subject:

"In the course of the liturgical year, the mysteries of faith and the rules of christian living are to be expounded in the homily from the sacred text" (c. 767, 1).

This is almost an exact quotation from the *Constitution on the Sacred Liturgy*, No. 52. Since it does not contain restrictive language, it should be interpreted primarily in the light of the major texts of the Vatican Council II rather than out of the subsequent instructions. The mind of the Council seems to have been to have the homily preached on sacred texts, but not necessarily those of the Mass of the day, and the new code has returned to this more inclusive understanding of the homily's content.

This broader interpretation would certainly be more in keeping with the entire historical development of the homily that was and is seen primarily as a means of promoting Christian living and an ever deepening union with Christ in the Eucharist. It is not a teaching aid that is consequent to the Scriptures of the day.

Since its purpose, then, is not to comment exclusively on the daily texts, the preacher is allowed to utilize other texts from time to time to fulfill the homily's primary purpose.

A proper theological understanding of the function of the homily within the eucharistic celebration can be helpful to contemporary preachers in using this particular form of communication to the greatest advantage for nourishing the faith life of their believing communities.

CONCLUSIONS

The first conclusion our explanation leads to is that there is no fixed and rigid format for the homily. As we have seen, there has been considerable variation in the homiletic form over the centuries, and different periods of the Church's history have used different models to define the homily. No single model has been preached consistently at all times.

Recognizing the diversity of homiletic forms in the past, we can exclude a few contemporary misconceptions about what a eucharistic homily is:

1. The homily is not an explanation of the liturgical rite, which should be clear in itself.
2. It is not exegesis of the Scripture text or, as sometimes happens, simply a repetition of the gospel pericope.
3. It does not simply identify and explain the liturgical theme of the day.
4. It is not a lecture or a reasoned discourse on a doctrinal subject unrelated to the eucharistic celebration.
5. It is not a moral exhortation to Christian behavior.
6. Finally, it is not appropriate to use the homily for special appeals, announcements, and the like.

The most effective way of achieving the goal of the eucharistic homily as renewed by the Second Vatican Council is for parish homilists to integrate their Sunday preaching into a total program of preaching, which includes the establishment of preaching opportunities for evangelization, catechesis, and didascalia. With such integration, the homily will be able to develop at the eucharistic celebrations those gospel elements that are preached in their own appropriate manner during other parish preaching events.

The parish, then, needs a master plan for a total program of parish preaching of which the eucharistic homily is only one element—a most important element, of course—but, nevertheless, only one element among many. The master plan of preaching for the homily should always be harmonious with the liturgical seasons and particular celebrations. Yet, at the same time, parish homilists need to be free to gear their preaching to the needs, hurts, fears, and loves of their parishioners. When homilists do this in a programmatic and progressive way under the ongoing graced action of the Holy Spirit, they will lead their flocks daily, weekly, and yearly into the fullness of our promised land.

NOTES

1. *Constitution on the Sacred Liturgy*, No. 10.

2. *Dogmatic Constitution on Divine Revelation*, No. 10.

3. Cf. 1 Samuel 3:1–18.

4. *St. Vladimir's Quarterly*, Vol. 4, No. 13.

5. Here we are particularly indebted, but not exclusively, to Thomas K. Carroll's brilliant study of the Christian homily: *Preaching the Word* (Wilmington, DE: Michael Glazier, Inc., 1984).

6. Cf. Acts 13:13–43.

Cf. John 14:10–12.

8. Carroll, op. cit., p. 43.

9. John Cardinal Newman, *Historical Sketches*, Vol. II (London: Longmans, Green, and Co., 1906), p. 234.

10. Carroll, op. cit., p. 208.

11. Pius XII, *Mediator Dei*, Vatican Library Translation (Washington, DC: National Catholic Welfare Conference), No. 100.

12. Cf. Polycarpus Rado, *Enchiridion Liturgicum* (Rome: Herder & Co., 1961), t. I, p. 534. Prior to the Second Vatican Council, liturgists considered all preaching at Mass a "secondary interruption" within the Mass. Ordination of bishops, religious professions, the blessing of spouses at marriage that took place within the Mass were "primary interruptions." The custom of introducing the homily with the sign of the cross or other introduction that sets the homily apart from the liturgical rhythm stems from this false understanding of its being a liturgical interruption and is still the practice of some priests today.

13. *Catholic Sunday Preaching* (Washington, DC: Word of God Institute, 1975).

Chapter Ten

The Integrated Preaching Program

In our exploration of preaching, we have seen that it is a complex ministry, which blends many diverse elements into a single, cohesive expression of truth and wisdom: the proclamation of the word of God. Because it is the communication of divine revelation, it is God's word; because it is uttered by human beings in time, it is very much a human word. Hence, all the literary rules that govern any human communication are applicable when we are considering the word of God.

We have seen, further, that the word of God is proclaimed by a preacher in order to give birth to and nourish faith in Jesus Christ. As a result, there are three levels, or phases, to the preaching, each of which depends on the level of faith that it is intended to arouse.

The complexity of such a ministry requires an integrating factor that necessarily is provided by the preacher. (He may, of course, be aided by advisors and councilors—the parish team.) The integrating factor is the preacher's personal gospel vision. This vision is the result of his own personal experience of Jesus as Lord, his scriptural and theological studies, his insights into the meaning of the gospel for his own life and the lives of others, his prayer and contemplation of the word of God.

As a result of his bringing together and interrelating these many elements, the preacher arrives at a Spirit-formed understanding of what the gospel is calling his community to be. It is not just an ideal; it is a true vision that can be incarnated by this gathering of people so that they are the faith community of love God wants them to be.

At the same time, the preacher is also aware of the reality of where his community is today. He recognizes how it falls short of the gospel as well as how it reflects the gospel. He knows he is forming a gathering of sinners in the process of becoming saints by the power of God's word.

St. Paul, a model for preachers of all ages, had a vision of what each of his communities should be like. They were not all exactly the same, nor were they communities of angels or faultless saints. They were real human beings with real problems and real sins that weakened the power of the gospel among them. Nevertheless, Paul knew what each could and should be by the power of God working in them.

For example, his community at Galatia was being heavily influenced by the preaching of the Judaizers who wanted to impose circumcision on the new converts to Christianity and make them follow the Mosaic law. Some members of the community were evidently accepting this false teaching and turning from the gospel. So in the Letter to the Galatians, Paul bluntly asks them:

"O stupid Galatians! Who has bewitched you? . . . Did you receive the Spirit from works of the law, or from faith in what you heard?" (Gal 3:1 ff.)

Then Paul goes on to give a moving teaching on the power of faith and what it effects in the lives of believers. He climaxes his teaching in the magnificent expression of sonship:

"As proof that you are children, God sent the spirit of his Son into our hearts, crying out, 'Abba, Father!' So you are no longer a slave but a child, and if a child then also an heir, through God" (Gal 4:6,7).

Like Paul, the contemporary preacher knows his community today is at point A, but he knows also that they are called to and can be at point B, perhaps in transit to a further point C. And the way the community is brought from A to B and even on to C is by the power of the word of God.

The preaching of the word of God will transform the community and incarnate the pastor-preacher's vision here and now, in flesh and blood, through the power of faith. When the preacher applies the healing word of God to his people's hurts as an "administrator of the new covenant," the Lord will transform them little by little into the perfect image of himself:

"All of us, gazing with unveiled face on the glory of the Lord, are being transformed into the same image from glory to glory, as from the Lord who is the Spirit" (2 Cor 3:18).

But of course such an transformation will not be instantaneous; transformation of such profundity does not happen overnight. Even Jesus did not transform his small band of apostles and disciples quickly. We human beings need time to mature as human beings and certainly as saints. The Scriptures are filled with texts that stress the importance of patience: God's patience with us, and our patience with God, others and, perhaps most of all, ourselves.[1]

Speaking of the delay of the coming of the Last Day, Peter writes:

"The Lord does not delay his promise, as some regard 'delay,' but is patient with you, not wishing that any should perish, but that all should come to repentance. But grow in grace and in the knowledge of our Lord and savior Jesus Christ" (2 Pt 3:9,18).

THE FIVE-YEAR MASTER PLAN OF PASSAGE

In order to be a patient and effective leader of his community on its pilgrimage of faith into the promised land, the preacher-pastor (and his team) needs a master plan of passage. He needs to organize his preaching of the word of God so that it both meets the real felt needs of his community and clearly and coherently communicates the entire gospel message.

We are calling this master plan of passage "The Integrated Preaching Program" because it interrelates all the preaching events in the parish to one another and to the people. The integrated preaching builds all the preaching events on each other in an ordered and developing way. Thus, when the parish preachers follow this methodology, the members of their community will be able to hear and, therefore, perceive the gospel message as a coherent and unified whole, which is relevant to their real-life situations.

Because of the complexity both of the word of God and the makeup of the communities, a convenient arrangement is to plan the preaching on a three- to five-year basis. There is a three-year lectionary cycle to consider, and many dioceses have terms for pastors of six years, so it is quite feasible to plan all the preaching in the parish no less than three and no more than five years in advance to achieve clear goals for the living out of the gospel in this community.

The principles that are given here regarding the formation of a parish community in faith can (with suitable adjustments) also be applied with equal effectiveness to the structuring of renewals, retreats, and preaching in religious communities. In fact, preaching according to a master plan will prove to be particularly helpful today to religious communities who seek to pass on the community's unique spiritual and apostolic tradition to both the members of the community and those they serve.

STRUCTURING THE INTEGRATED PREACHING PROGRAM

There are four basic steps to the structuring of the program:

Step 1. *Identify the felt needs or experienced hurts of the community.*

In Chapter Four, we pointed out how important it is for the pastoral team to be sensitive to the needs, experiences, hungers, and hurts of the parish community they serve. In addition, we suggested surveying the parish and using broad-based sociological findings to determine the profile of a parish.

Step 2. *Identify the basic insight or insights that can be applied to heal each hurt.*

The schema in Chapter Four shows how specific themes are related to specific needs, but it also shows how the major themes of revelation can be interrelated in an integrated preaching program. Using this schema could be helpful to a pastor in lining up the felt need with the appropriate insight to see the areas on which his preaching should focus during any given period of time.

Step 3. *Relate steps 1 and 2 to one another in a way that will result in community growth.*

This, of course, is the heart of the program, and the step that demands the greatest amount of creative effort.

Step 4. *Identify all the opportunities that can be used to preach the word, using any format, and that can be done by any minister of the word in the community under the leadership of the chief preacher.*

The most obvious opportunity to preach the word of God to the community is the Sunday homily. Yet it allows for only eight to twelve hours of Christian message a year.

If a preacher, for example, were to preach a ten-minute homily forty-eight Sundays a year, he would be able to communicate only eight hours of Christian message to his community by eucharistic preaching in the course of a year. If he were to extend the homily to fifteen minutes, he would still only preach a total of twelve hours in the course of year. And since not all of his parishioners will be there every Sunday he preaches, it means that he is giving many of his parishioners even less of the gospel message.

Now compare the preacher's eucharistic preaching time to that which families give to the viewing of television. Most homes have their television on eight hours in the course of a single day, that is, more viewing television in a single day than they hear preaching in the course of the entire year. The competition for influence between the two, therefore, is as unbalanced as it is intense, and the Sunday homily alone cannot really do much to shape a way of life in those circumstances. Fortunately, there are many other opportunities to preach in a parish.

There are daily Masses, funerals, marriages, baptisms, anointings, and reconciliation. Parishes also conduct retreats, mission/renewals, days of recollection, and Forty Hours. In addition, there are special programs, such as the Rite of Christian Initiation of Adults and evangelization.

But all of these in no way exhaust the opportunities to preach. Each parish holds meetings of its administrative staff, pastoral team, parish council, finance committee, liturgy committee, and the choir. At these meetings, the pastor can communicate the word of God either formally or informally.

In addition, all parishes devote major resources of personnel and money to their catechetical programs for youth, which include training and planning meetings for the teachers in the programs. There may be special CYO and sports programs for teenagers, along with other youth-centered activities, which also have meetings where the pastor can preach, even briefly.

Special parish groups provide opportunities for preaching at their meetings, such as the charismatics at their prayer meetings and Bible sharing groups at their sessions.

There are other organizations that have meetings at which the pastor can preach, either briefly or at some length: Marriage Encounter, Cursillo, Pre-Cana, the altar society, the altar servers, the Knights of Columbus, Legion of Mary, St. Vincent De Paul Society, and many others.

Counseling occupies much of a pastor's time, but it can really be a preaching event. Finally, parish bulletins and newsletters can be used effectively to support the oral communication of the word of God by recommending additional reading, for example, and exchanging parishioners' insights through letters.

When all these activities are added together, there are many hours in the year when the parish preacher(s) can proclaim the word of God. When the proclamation is done on an organized basis, these many opportunities, collectively, will enable the preacher to have a great effect on the shaping of the community of faith.

Consider one segment of a possible integrated preaching program for a particular parish. The pastor in this case has decided that he will design an integrated preaching program that will span a period of five years. The following is a description of one small segment of his total program: preaching during the four weeks of Advent.

Step 1. *Identify the felt needs or experienced hurts of the community.*

The pastor begins by analyzing his parish and discovers that the people in the parish are reserved, tend to be rather shy with one another, and, at times, even unfriendly. Instead of welcoming newcomers into the parish, they make them feel like intruders.

Lacking social interaction within the community, there is not much sense of being a community and little community spirit. Few take part in community activities, so that the pastor has great difficulty in persuading people to undertake necessary community projects or volunteer for special jobs. As a result, the parish does not have much outreach to the broader secular community; it has no programs on behalf of social justice or broad community issues, such as education. Consequently, the parish has little influence socially or politically.

Furthermore, the parishioners are very reluctant to listen to, much less embrace, new ideas. In fact, they resist change and complain bitterly when any innovation is proposed. This attitude is particularly evident in matters of liturgy; they refuse to make any effort to mature in liturgical celebration, and the liturgy committee has become a battleground between self-styled "liberals" and "conservatives." All in all, the pastor has found his community of faith to be a very difficult one to lead. It is not attracting new members, while the old-timers remain distant from community life. The young people, in particular, are turned off by the attitudes of their elders, and some have left the community to join Protestant Churches.

However, through careful analysis, the pastor has come to recognize that all these diverse symptoms really point to a single basic cause: Many members of the parish community really lack a healthy sense of self-identity. He has discovered that many, even those who seem secure and successful, suffer deeply from a fear that others will reject them.

Step 2. *Identify the basic insight or insights that can be applied to heal each hurt.*

Although there are a variety of reasons why this phenomenon exists in the particular parish, the pastor has come to realize that he can cut quickly to the heart of the matter by proclaiming God's love for each of them.

The revelation of God's infinite and abiding love for his chosen people is articulated theologically and scripturally in the Catholic tradition by the doctrine of predestination. Protestantism, especially Calvinism, has attached other notes to predestination, such as reprobation, but for Catholics, predestination is a doctrinal development of the revelation found in such scriptural texts as Psalm 139, Romans 5, etc.

This revelation of the divine choice is expressed with particular poignancy in Ephesians 1:3–14, previously cited:

"Blessed be the God and Father of our Lord Jesus Christ, who has blessed us in Christ with every spiritual blessing in the heavens, as he chose us in him, before the foundation of the world, to be holy and without blemish before him."

Furthermore, the pastor sees the incarnation of Jesus as a very particular and practical manifestation of divine choice. Hence, he decides that as part of his integrated preaching program—his master plan—he will devote all four weeks of Advent that lead into Christmas and Epiphany to preaching on predestination. This theme, of course, is appropriate to the liturgical season and suitable to use in conjunction with the lectionary texts.

Step 3. Relate steps 1 and 2 to one another in a way that will result in community growth.

Having the proper appreciation of Christian revelation, and aware of its value for those who lack feelings of self-worth, perhaps due to enslavement to sins of one kind or another, the pastor-preacher works creatively to relate the one doctrinal theme of predestination with its numerous manifestations in Christian life to the felt needs of the community he has identified in Number 1. During Advent, then, all the preaching opportunities will reflect that single theme.

Step 4. Identify all the opportunities that can be used to preach the word, using any format, and that can be done by any minister of the word in the community under the leadership of the chief preacher.

The pastor will preach on that theme in the Sunday homilies for all four Sundays of Advent. Because he usually preaches for fifteen minutes, in his four Sunday homilies he will have a full hour to preach on predestination.

Furthermore, all his daily homilies during Advent will also be on predestination. His daily homilies are only five minutes long, a time limitation made necessary by the work schedules of those attending Mass. Nevertheless, because he will be preaching twenty homilies during that period of time, he will have the opportunity to preach one hour and forty minutes on a central Catholic doctrine, predestination, to a very important, spiritually strong, and faith-filled segment of his parish community.

During Advent, the liturgy committee of the parish will be meeting to plan the Christmas liturgies. At these meetings, the pastor will preach to them about predestination as a way of helping them design the most appropriate liturgical celebrations to evoke a response of faith from their parish community.

During this same period, the choir and guitar groups of the parish meet to plan and rehearse the music for the Christmas liturgies. The preacher will use some of their meeting time to preach on (talk on, address) predestination. He may relate his preaching to this group as a means of helping them select appropriate music for the liturgies, but the pastor-preacher will also address their needs as Christians who seek to deepen their relationship with the Lord.

The preacher has established a good relationship with the altar servers; in addition to instructing them in the service of the altar, he is their spiritual advisor, friend, and party-giver. At their regular meeting, which is conducted under rather severe time restrictions, he takes ten minutes to talk to them seriously about predestination. Subsequently, he knows he will be asked questions about his presentation in informal sessions or in ordinary conversation. These questions will enable him to expand on his teaching, which the lack of time so severely restricted.

The pastor-preacher will have a major meeting with the religion teachers to set up a religion program so that all the religion classes taught during Advent will communicate the same theme of predestination.

Setting up the program will mean that the preacher will have to teach the catechists the correct doctrine of predestination, if they are not already versed in it. While it may require a great deal of personal research and reflection on the part of both the pastor and his catechists, when they have mastered this one teaching, it will have lasting effects on their teaching in the future, as well as for their own personal lives of faith.

The preacher will also meet with the teen organization to help them plan their annual Christmas party; during that time he will preach (talk to them) on predestination. This will have to be a very informal presentation, with much give-and-take discussion; nevertheless, it is still a form of preaching and a most potent one for the youth group.

When the party is actually held, the preacher will give a welcoming address; it will be brief and (one may hope) witty, but it, too, will be a communication of predestination adapted to meet the listening needs of his young audience.

The parish's charismatic prayer group will have four prayer meetings during Advent. At two of them, the preacher will have the opportunity to give a major teaching on predestination to the whole prayer group. In addition, he will meet with the prayer group leaders and prepare them to give two major teachings themselves to the group during this period of time. Hence, between the preacher and the leaders, the prayer group will receive an in-depth explanation of the Catholic understanding of predestination.

When the Altar Society has its monthly meeting during Advent, the preacher will use thirty minutes of their meeting to preach on predestination. The Society is well-disposed to listen to regular teachings by the preacher and looks forward to these moments of special instruction arranged to meet their needs.

Marriage Encounter will have one meeting during the Advent season, and the preacher will have forty-five minutes during this meeting to speak. He, again, will preach on predestination with particular emphasis on how God's love for us finds expression in the human relationships within the family.

The Knights of Columbus hold an annual Christmas Dinner as one of their major social events of the year. The pastor is always asked to be the emcee because he is a very entertaining after-dinner speaker. During this speech, laced with his customary witticisms, which are truly entertaining, he will preach on (talk about) predestination. In spite of the seriousness and profundity of the topic, the pastor's skill and preparation will make the talk appropriate to the lightness and joy of the occasion. Nevertheless, a basic doctrine and a healing one for this community will be proclaimed.

During the four weeks of Advent, therefore, by carefully organizing his ideas and fitting them to meet the various preaching occasions available to him, the pastor-preacher will be able to address all the special groups that make up his total Christian community: young, mature, male, female, single, married. Furthermore, all who hear the preaching will have both sufficient information and motivation to discuss God's love in the privacy of their homes as well as in public.

For instance, at breakfast, the morning after the Knights of Columbus' annual Christmas dinner, when the family is discussing the previous night's events, the Knight and his wife find that their son, an altar server, has also heard how much God loves his people in his altar server meeting. Their daughter, a member of the guitar group, adds that she, too, heard the same message. The wife, because of the more developed teaching she received at the Altar Society's meeting, is able to clarify some of the points in the doctrine the family did not have an opportunity to grasp in the less complete teachings at the briefer or less formal meetings. When the next-door neighbor, a charismatic, drops by, he contributes some significant insights into the meaning of the doctrine that came out of the prayer group's faith sharing.

In other words, the interaction of the persons of the community with one another in their homes as well as in the activities of the parish reveals to the entire community how God's love for his people is made incarnate in Jesus Christ. The entire parish, therefore, becomes focused on one powerful insight of the parish preacher. This insight can be presented in a variety of forms under widely diverse conditions; yet, the revelation will be coherently proclaimed and bear rich fruit in the lives of all the hearers through the power of the word of God. Christmas and Epiphany will be great celebrations in the parish this year. They will be significant celebrations in the parish's move from point A to point B.

Moreover, this one, fundamental and consoling teaching will lay the groundwork for subsequent teachings that the pastor has outlined for himself for the entire five-year period. When a preacher plans his preaching like a teacher who plans his classroom activities in the light of the school year, he greatly increases the effectiveness of his preaching of the word of God.

EASING THE BURDEN

Using an integrated preaching program significantly eases the burden of weekly and daily eucharistic homilizing. One of the major difficulties homilists have is just getting an idea for the Sunday homily. This is because they so often try to come up with a new, distinct and, sometimes, even fanciful idea week after week. It really means the preacher has to start from scratch every week, which can be an exhausting process. The integrated preaching program, on the other hand, allows the homilist to build one idea or theme upon preceding ideas and themes in a logical and emotionally apt sequence.

Furthermore, an idea may come to the preacher that may not be appropriate for an immediate sermon, but when he knows what he is going to preach on six months in the future, he can preserve his good ideas for development at another, more suitable time in his program. With the integrated preaching program, therefore, the search for the idea has been completed even before the homilist begins his creative process for an individual homily.

It is true, to design the basic plan may take time, but once the topics have been selected and the sequence of development has been decided on, the ideas will be interrelated to one another, and the preaching of the Christian message can be done in a logical and developing manner that will serve as the focus of parish growth in faith for years.

This also means the preacher will be able to avoid repeating things he has said many times previously. He can be sure that his people are being given the opportunity to grow in the experience of the mystery of Christ, moving from A to B to C.

THE PREACHER'S GROWTH
There is one last advantage to using the integrated preaching program for parish preaching. It assures the preacher's own growth in Christ. Planning his preaching for extended periods of time demands of the preacher, his preaching associates, and his community constant study and updating. The integrated preaching program gives the preacher the opportunity to explore new aspects of divine revelation, the Church's tradition, and current events and keeps him theologi-

cally alive and scripturally vital. Because of this, the parish community will be in no danger of being held back from growth in Christ because the preacher himself has not grown in his own understanding of the gospel.

NOTES

1. Cf. 1 Corinthians 13:4; James 5:7; and 1 Peter 1:5–12.

Bibliography

Abbott., Walter M., S. J. (gen. ed.). *The Documents of Vatican II*. Tr. ed. Joseph Gallagher. New York: Guild Press, 1966.

Augustine. *Confessions*. New York: Sheed and Ward, 1943.

Baars, Conrad W., and Anna A. Terruwe. *Healing the Unaffirmed: Recognizing Deprivation Neurosis*. New York: Alba House, 1976.

Barr, James. *Fundamentalism*. Philadelphia: Westminster Press, 1978. A theological examination by a British Old Testament scholar.

Bausch, William J. *Traditions, Tensions, Transitions in Ministry*. Mystic, CT: Twenty-Third Publications, 1982.

Bellah, Robert N., et al. *Habits of the Heart: Individualism and Commitment in American Life*. Berkeley: University of California Press, 1985.

Burke, John, O.P. *Gospel Power: Toward the Revitalization of Preaching*. New York: Alba House, 1978.

———. "Must We Preach the Lectionary?" *Today's Parish* (April/May 1982).

Burke, John, O.P. (ed.). *A New Look at Preaching*. Wilmington, DE: Michael Glazier, Inc., 1983. Significant contributions to a contemporary articulation of the theology of preaching by Walter J. Burghardt, S.J.; Elisabeth Schussler Fiorenza; Raymond E. Brown, S.S.;

James M. Reese, O.S.F.S.; Edward E. Braxton; Fred B. Craddock; William J. Hill, O.P.; James A. Forbes, Jr.; Leander E. Keck; Gerard S. Sloyan.

——. *The Sunday Homily*. Washington, DC: Thomist Press, 1966.

Carlen, Claudia, I.H.M. (ed.). *The Papal Encyclicals*. 5 vols. New York: McGrath Publishing Company, 1981.

Carroll, Thomas K. *Preaching the Word*. Wilmington, DE: Michael Glazier, Inc., 1984. (Paperback.) A history of the homily among the Fathers.

Clark, Walter H. *The Psychology of Religion*. New York: Macmillan, 1968.

Code of Canon Law in English Translation. London: Collins Liturgical Publications, 1983.

Craddock, Fred B. *As One With Authority*. 3d ed. Nashville, TN: Abingdon, 1979.

Crum, Milton. *Manual on Preaching*. Valley Forge, PA: Judson Press, 1977. A methodology of sermon construction.

Dodd, C. H. *The Apostolic Preaching and Its Developments*. New York: Harper and Row, 1964. A brilliant scriptural analysis of the earliest preaching in the Church.

Dolan, Jay P. *Catholic Revivalism: The American Experience 1830–1900*. Notre Dame, IN: Notre Dame Press, 1978.

Dominican Media Report: A Task Force Study in Religious Broadcasting. Washington, DC: Word of God Institute, unpublished.

Dulles, Avery. *A Testimonial to Grace*. New York: Sheed and Ward, 1946.

Falwell, Jerry, (ed). *The Fundamental Phenomenon: The*

Resurgence of Conservative Christianity. Garden City, NY: Doubleday, 1981.

Fichtner, Joseph, O.S.C. *To Stand and Speak for Christ: A Theology of Preaching*. New York: Alba House, 1981.

Gallup, George W. *Emerging Trends*. Princeton: Princeton Religion Research Center (ten issues per year). Reports on contemporary sociological research in religious issues.

Gelpi, Donald L., S.J. *Charism and Sacrament: A Theology of Christian Conversion*. New York: Paulist Press, 1976.

Gillis, Raymond Franklin. *The Role of Feedback in Preaching: Some Methods for Acquiring Feedback From the Congregation*. Ann Arbor, MI: University Microfilms International, 1983.

Graham, William H. "Practicing the Art of Preaching," *Church* (Spring, 1986).

Griffin, Emilie. *Turning: Reflections on the Experience of Conversion*. Garden City, NY: Doubleday Image Books, 1982.

Griffiths, Dom Bede. *The Golden String*. Springfield, IL: Templegate, 1980.

Hadden, Jeffrey K, and Charles E. Swann. *Prime Time Preachers: The Rising Power of Televangelism*. Reading, MA: Addison-Wesley Publishing Co. A must for understanding contemporary religious broadcasting.

Hoge, Dean R. *Converts, Dropouts, Returnees*. New York: Pilgrim Press, 1981.

Jabusch, Willard F. *The Person in the Pulpit/Preaching as Caring*. Nashville, TN: Parthenon Press, Abingdon, 1980. Paperback.

John Paul II. *Catechesis in Our Time*. (*Catechesi Tradendae*). Boston: Daughters of St. Paul, 1979.

————. *Redeemer of Mankind* (*Redemptor Hominis*). Washington, DC: United States Catholic Conference, 1979.

————. *Rich in Mercy* (*Dives in Misericordia*). Hales Corners, WI: Priests of the Sacred Heart, 1980.

————. *Reconciliation and Penance* (*Reconciliatio et Paenitentia*). Vatican City: Libreria Editrice Vaticana, 1984.

John XXIII. *Mater et Magistra*. New York: The America Press, 1961.

————. "Peace on Earth." ("Pacem in Terris") in Peter Riga, *Peace on Earth: A Commentary on Pope John's Encyclical*. New York: Herder and Herder, 1963.

Keck, Leander E. *The Bible in the Pulpit*. Nashville, TN: Abingdon Press, 1978.

Keegan, Terence J., O.P. *Interpreting the Bible: A Popular Introduction to Biblical Hermeneutics*. Mahwah, NJ: Paulist Press, 1985. Paperback. An excellent updating of biblical criticism that stresses the role of the Church-reader in arriving at the meaning of Scripture.

Leo XIII. "Rerum Novarum" ("On Capital and Labor"), in Claudia Carlen, I.H.M. (ed.), *The Papal Encyclicals*. Vol 2, 1878–1903, pp. 241–261. New York: McGrath Publishing Company, 1981.

Lewis, C. S. *Surprised by Joy: The Shape of My Early Life*. New York: Harcourt, Brace and World, 1955.

Marsden, George M. *Fundamentalism and American Culture: The Shaping of Twentieth Century Evangelism, 1870–1925*. New York: Oxford University Press, 1980. A comprehensive history.

McNamara, R. F. *Catholic Sunday Preaching*. Washington, DC: Word of God Institute, 1975. Paperback. A history of the homily in the United States.

Merton, Thomas. *The Seven Storey Mountain*. New York: Harcourt, Brace, 1948.

National Conference of Catholic Bishops. *Fulfilled in Your Hearing: The Homily in the Sunday Assembly*. Washington, DC: USCC Publications Office, 1982. Very practical guidelines and suggestions for planning, preparing, and preaching the Sunday homily.

Nock, A.D. *Conversion*. London: Oxford University Press, 1933 [1972].

Notre Dame Study of Catholic Parish Life. South Bend, IN: Institute for Pastoral and Social Ministry and the Center for the Study of Contemporary Society, University of Notre Dame. Phased reports.

Oates, Wayne E. *The Psychology of Religion*. Waco, TX: Word Books, 1973.

Paul VI. *On Evangelization in the Modern World (Evangelii Nuntiandi)*. (Dec. 8, 1975.) Washington, DC: USCC Publications Office, 1975. A landmark teaching on evangelization.

Pius XII. *Mediator Dei*. Washington, DC: National Catholic Welfare Conference, 1947.

Rauff, Edward A. *Why People Join the Church*. Washington, DC: Glenmary Research Center and New York: Pilgrim Press, 1979. Paperback.

Reese, James M., O.S.F.S. *Experiencing the Good News: The New Testament as Communication*. Wilmington, DE: Michael Glazier, 1984.

Religion in America. Princeton, NJ: Princeton Religion Research Center and Gallup Poll. Annual sociological reports.

A Review of the Principal Trends in the Life of the Catholic Church in the United States. Washington, DC: United States Catholic Conference, 1974.

Sects or New Religious Movements: Pastoral Challenge. A Report to Episcopal Conferences issued by the Vatican Secretariat to Promote Christian Unity, May 3, 1986.

Tomczak, Larry. *Clap Your Hands*. Plainsfield, NJ: Logos International, 1973.

Tugwell, Simon, O.P. *The Way of the Preacher*. Springfield, IL: Templegate, 1979. Paperback. Written from a Dominican perspective, and an excellent exploration of preaching as a gift.

Vitz, Paul C. *Psychology as Religion: The Cult of Self-Worship*. Grand Rapids, MI: Wm. B. Eerdmans, 1977. A most helpful book for coming to understand the psychological milieu of contemporary America.

Acknowledgments

International Commission on English in the Liturgy for excerpts from the English translation of *Documents on the Liturgy, 1963–1979: Conciliar, Papal, and Curial Texts*, © 1982, International Committee on English in the Liturgy, Inc. All rights reserved.

The New Yorker for "Notes and Comment" from *The Talk of the Town*, December 22, 1980 issue. Reprinted by permission; © 1980 The New Yorker Magazine, Inc.

United States Catholic Conference Publications for use of brief quotations from *A Review of the Principal Trends in the Life of the Catholic Church in the United States*, 1974. John Paul II, "Holy Thursday Letter to Priests," *Origins*, Vol. 15, No. 42, 685–691. Washington, DC: NC Documentary Service: John Paul II, *Redeemer of Mankind (Redemptor Hominis)*, 1979. National Conference of Catholic Bishops, *Fulfilled in Your Hearing: The Homily in the Sunday Assembly*, 1982, and *The Challenge of Peace: God's Promise and Our Response*, 1983. Paul VI, *On Evangelization in the Modern World (Evangelii Nuntiandi)*, 1975.

Sheed and Ward for quotations from St. Augustine *Confessions* by F. J. Sheed; *A Testimonial to Grace* by Avery Dulles. Used with permission of Sheed and Ward, 115 E. Armour Blvd., Kansas City, MO 64141.

Collins Publishers for permission to quote from *Code of Canon Law*, © 1983 The Canon Law Society. Reproduced with permission of the publishers.

Libreria Editrice Vaticana for permission to reproduce excerpts from John Paul II, *Reconciliation and Penance*.

Index

God
harmony with, 190–191
union with, 180–182, 187–191, 201

Good News, 11, 21, 78, 165, 222

Good News preaching, 96

Good Samaritan, parable of the, 102, 103

Gospel, 71, 202
Church's preaching of the, 28
communicating the, 146–147
and felt need, scheme for, 115, 116–117
and felt need, relating to, 114–118
preacher's ability to communicate the, 41
preaching as, 1
preaching the, 91–118
preaching communicates the, 40–41

Gospel wisdom, 33

Grace, 32, 33, 42
experience of, 22

Greek homily, 224, 225

Gregory the Great, Pope, 226

Griffin, Emilie, 134

Group reflections, 113

Guilt as a felt need, 116

H
Happiness, 80

Harmony
inner, 189–190
religious, 209
social, 209
with God, 190–191

Hehir, J. Brian, 105

High Middle Ages, 4

Hill, William J., 22

Himmer, Charles-Marie, 229